John R. Howard

Patriotic Nuggets

John R. Howard

Patriotic Nuggets

ISBN/EAN: 9783743317949

Manufactured in Europe, USA, Canada, Australia, Japa

Cover: Foto ©Suzi / pixelio.de

Manufactured and distributed by brebook publishing software
(www.brebook.com)

John R. Howard

Patriotic Nuggets

Patriotic Nuggets

FRANKLIN   WASHINGTON   JEFFERSON
WEBSTER   LINCOLN   BEECHER

Gathered by JOHN R. HOWARD

NEW YORK:
FORDS, HOWARD, & HULBERT

NOTE.

There can be no question but that war is a stimulant of patriotism. A majority of the men whose words are here gathered wrote or spoke under that tremendous pressure. And yet, the sum of their counsels is to avoidance of war, towards aspiration for a national greatness developing out of the arts of peace.

Naturally, a reader familiar with the writings of any of them will miss here many favorite passages : the scope of the compilation being necessarily limited. The attentive reader, however, will be interested to trace herein the vital germs of our entire American history, the swift and strong expansion of which furnished the world with unceasing wonder. Webster's pictures of the Colonial settlements : the sentiments of Franklin, Washington and Jefferson, showing their love of the Mother-Country, indignation at her oppressions of the Colonies, ardor for

Revolutionary success, sagacity in framing the new government, wisdom in its administration, and appeals for increasing devotion to the Union, in which alone they found the source of permanent strength and prosperity, —these all stand out with striking distinctness. There follows the intermediate period of incubating Nullification and Secession, with Webster's teachings of national honor in finance, and his grand arguments for the Constitution and the Union, so powerful in consolidating the national sentiment, in preparation for the war whose horrors he foretold.

After this, the deluge of Secession and Rebellion, set forth in Lincoln's clear, terse English and with his inimitable force of logic and good sense. The volume closes with Beecher, who ranged from the Compromise day of Clay in 1850, through the Anti-slavery struggles, the War, and Reconstruction, down to the death of Grant in 1885—a splendid array of reason and eloquence.

The notable thing about these men—rev-

olutionary prophets all, except Webster—is
their con‌servatism, both in thought and in
expression. Even their most strenuous appeals to sentiment are based on a rational
setting forth of facts, compelling confidence
in their conclusions. Their utterances of
patriotic fervor are at the opposite pole
from the demagogy of partisanship. And,
aside from their inculcations of national
honor, virtue, justice, the education of intelligence, freedom from foreign entangle-
ments, and independent friendliness to
other nations, perhaps the most valuable
lesson for the present generation is a realiza-
tion of the growth and importance of the
federal union of the several States. It began
weakly; was subject to attack, first insidi-
ous, then violent; survived after a mighty
struggle; and now seems to us a matter of
course, as permanently established:—but,
from the outset to the end, whether for peaceful growth or warlike force, these clear-eyed
prophets saw its value, and proclaimed it
with effective iteration. While yet the
States, like the planets, hold each its in-

dependent orbit, the system stands for " Our Country, our whole Country, one and indivisible."

For the text of the excerpts, the compiler has depended chiefly on the following: FRANKLIN,—*Complete Works*, Ed. by John Bigelow (Putnam); WASHINGTON,—*Writings*, Ed. by Worthington A. Ford (Putnam); JEFFERSON,—*Writings*, Ed. by Paul L. Ford (Putnam); WEBSTER,—*Great Speeches*, Ed. by E. C. Whipple (Little, Brown & Co.); LINCOLN, *Complete Works*, Ed. by John G. Nicolay and John Hay (Century Co.); BEECHER, *Patriotic Addresses*, Ed. by J. R. Howard (Fords, Howard, & Hulbert.)

CONTENTS.

BENJAMIN FRANKLIN.

The sage whom two worlds claim ; the man, disputed by the history of the sciences and the history of
empires. . . .one of the greatest men who ever served
the cause of liberty and of philosophy.—MIRABEAU,
in the French National Assembly.

To Lord Kames.
London, January, 1760.

o one can more sincerely rejoice than I
on the reduction of Canada, and this not
ely as I am a colonist, but as I am a
on. I have long been of the opinion,
the foundations of the future grandeur
and stability of the British Empire lie in
America : and though like other foundations,
they are low and little seen, they are nevertheless broad, and strong enough to support
the greatest political structure human wisdom has ever yet erected. I am therefore
by no means for restoring Canada [to the
French]. If we keep it, all the Country
from St. Lawrence to Mississippi will in
another century be filled with British people,

Britain itself will become vastly more populous, by the immense increase of its commerce ; the Atlantic Sea will be covered
with your trading ships ; and your naval
powers, thence continually increasing, will
extend your influences round the whole globe
and over the world !

To M. Dubourg.
London, October 2, 1770.

We of the colonies have never insisted
that we ought to be exempt from contribut-
ing to the common expenses necessary to support the prosperity of the empire. We only
assert that, having parliaments of our own,
and not having representatives in that of
Great Britain, our parliaments are the only
judges of what we can and what we ought
to contribute in this case ; and that the
English Parliament has no right to take our
money without our consent. . . . I have,
indeed, no doubt that the parliament of
England will finally abandon its pretensions
and leave us to the peaceable enjoyment of
our rights and privileges.

To Thomas Cushing, Speaker of the Assembly of Massachusetts Bay. Reporting his conversation with Lord Dartmouth.—London, 6 May, 1773.

Were I as much an Englishman as I am an American, and ever so desirous of establishing the authority of Parliament, I protest to your Lordship, I cannot conceive of a single step the Parliament can take to increase it that will not tend to diminish it, and after abundance of mischief they must finally lose it.

To Thomas Cushing.—
London, 5 Jan., 1774.

I shall continue to do all I possibly can this winter to make an accommodation of our differences ; but my hopes are small. Divine Providence first infatuates the power it designs to ruin.

To the Printer of the London Public Advertiser (Anonymously sent), 1774.

Surely the great commerce of this nation with the Americans is of too much importance to be risked in a quarrel which has no foundation but ministerial pique and obstinacy! . . . . Did ever any tradesman succeed who attempted to drub customers into his shop?

TO JAMES BOWDOIN.—

London, 25 Feb., 1775.

If we continue firm and united, and resolutely persist in the non-consumption agreement, this adverse ministry cannot probably stand another year . . . . The eyes of all Christendom are upon us, and our honor as a people is become a matter of the utmost consequence to be taken care of. If we tamely give up our rights in this contest, a century to come will not restore us in the opinion of the world; we shall be stamped with the character of dastards, poltroons and fools. . . . Present inconveniences are therefore to be born with fortitude, and better times expected.

TO MR. STRAHAN (King's Printer).—

Philadelphia, 7 July, 1775.

Mr. STRAHAN :—You are a member of Parliament, and one of that majority which has doomed my country to destruction. You have begun to burn our towns and murder our people. Look upon your hands; they are stained with the blood of your relations! You and I were long friends ; you are now my enemy, and I am

Yours,

B. FRANKLIN.

To LORD HOWE.—
Philadelphia, July 20, 1776.

To me it seems, that neither the obtaining or retaining of any trade, however valuable soever, is an object for which men may justly spill each other's blood: that the true and sure means of extending and securing commerce is the goodness and cheapness of commodities : and that the profit of no trade can ever be equal to the expense of compelling it and of holding it, by fleets and armies.

To SAMUEL COOPER.—
Paris, May 1, 1777.

Those who live under arbitrary power do nevertheless approve of liberty, and wish for it; they almost despair of receiving it in Europe; they read the translations of our separate Colony constitutions with rapture: .... Hence it is a common observation here that our cause is *the cause of all mankind*, and that we are fighting for their liberty in defending our own. It is a glorious task assigned us by Providence, which has, I trust, given us spirit and virtue equal to it, and will at last crown it with success.

To CHAS. DE WEISSENTEIN [a secret agent of England].—Passy, July 1, 1778.

You think we flatter ourselves and are deceived into an opinion that England *must* acknowledge our independency. We, on the other hand, think you flatter yourselves in imagining such an acknowledgment a vast boon. . . . We have never asked it of you; we only tell you that you can have no treaty with us but as an independent state; and you may please yourselves and your children with the rattle of the right to govern us, as long as you have done with your King's being King of France, without giving us the least concern, if you do not attempt to exercise it.

To James Lovell.—
Passy, July 22, 1778.

The taking of unfair advantage of a neighbor's necessities, though attended with temporary success, always breeds bad blood.

Information to Those Who Would Remove to America.—1782.

In Europe it [birth] has indeed its value; but it is a commodity that cannot be carried to a worse market than America, where people do not inquire concerning a stranger, *What is he?* but, *What can he do?* If he has any useful art, he is welcome.

Industry and constant employment are great preservatives of the morals and the virtue of a nation.

To the Bishop of St. Asaph, Dr. Shipley.—Passy, March 17, 1783.

Let us now forgive and forget. Let each country seek its advancement in its own internal advantages of arts and agriculture, not in retarding and preventing the prosperity of the other. America will, with God's blessing, become a great and happy country ; and England, if she has at length gained wisdom, will have gained something more valuable, and more essential to her prosperity, than all she has lost.

TO ROBERT R. LIVINGSTONE.—

Passy, 22 July, 1783.

I have seen so much embarrassment and so little advantage in the restraining and compulsive systems, that I feel myself strongly inclined to believe that a state which leaves her ports open to all the world upon equal terms will by that means have foreign commodities cheaper, sell its own productions dearer, and be, as a whole, the most prosperous.

[Our constitutions] are much admired by the politicians here. It is particularly a matter of wonder that, in the midst of a cruel war raging in the bowels of our country, our sages should have the firmness of mind to sit down calmly and form such complete plans of government.

To Sir Joseph Banks.—
Passy, 27 July, 1783.

In my opinion *there never was a good war or a bad peace.* What vast additions to the conveniences and comforts of living might mankind have acquired, if the money spent on wars had been employed in works of public utility!

To David Hartley (One of the English Peace Commissioners).—
Passy, 6 Sept., 1783.

We are more thoroughly an enlightened people, with respect to our political interests, than perhaps any other under heaven. Every man among us reads. . . . Our domestic misunderstandings, when we have them, are of small extent. . . . The great body of intelligence among our people surrounds and overpowers our petty dissensions, as the sun's great mass of fire diminishes and destroys his spots. Do not, therefore, any longer delay the evacuation of New York, in the vain hope of a new revolution in your favor.

There is no truth more clear to me than this, that the great interest of our two countries is a thorough reconciliation.

To JOSIAH QUINCY.—
Passy, 11 Sept., 1783.

I lament with you the many mischiefs, the injustice, the corruption of manners, etc., that attended a depreciating currency. It is some consolation to me, that I washed my hands of that evil by predicting it in Congress, and proposing means that would have been effectual to prevent it, if they had been adopted.

To THE PRESIDENT OF CONGRESS.—
Passy, 13 Sept., 1783.

Our safety consists in a steady adherence to our friends, and our reputation in a faithful regard to treaties.

To ROBERT MORRIS.—
Passy, 5 Dec., 1783.

I see, in some resolutions of town meetings, a remonstrance against giving Congress the power to take, as they call it, the people's money out of their pockets, though only to pay the interest and principal of debts duly contracted. They seem to mistake the point. Money, justly due from the people, is their creditors' money, and no longer the money of the people.

THE IMPOLICY OF WAR.

I agreed with you perfectly in your disapprobation of war .... I think it wrong in point of human prudence, for whatever advantage one nation would obtain from another. . . . it would be much cheaper to purchase such advantage with ready money, than to pay the expense of acquiring it by war. . . . It seems to me that if statesmen had a little more arithmetic, or were more accustomed to calculations, wars would be much less frequent.

TO CHAS. THOMSON, Secretary of Congress.
—Passy, 13 May, 1783.

Thus the great and hazardous enterprise we have been engaged in, is, God be praised, happily completed, an event I hardly expected I should live to see. A few years of peace, well employed, will restore and increase our strength, but our future safety will depend on our union and virtue.

TO B. VAUGHAN.—
Passy, 14 March, 1785.

Justice is as strictly due between neighbor nations as between neighbor citizens. A highwayman is as much a robber when he plunders in a gang as when single ; and a nation that makes an unjust war is only a *great gang.*

ADDRESS TO THE CONSTITUTIONAL CONVENTION.—Sept., 1787.

I confess that I do not entirely approve of this Constitution at present ; but, Sir, I am not sure I shall never approve of it ; for, having lived long, I have experienced many instances of being obliged, by better information and fuller consideration, to change opinions even on important subjects which I once thought right, but found to be otherwise. . . . Though many private persons think almost as highly of their own infallibility as that of their [religious] sect, few express it so naturally as a certain French lady, who in a little dispute with her sister, said : "But I meet with nobody but myself that is *always* in the right." In these sentiments, Sir, I agree to this Constitution. . . . [I] doubt, too, whether any convention we can obtain may be able to make a better Constitution. . . . On the whole, Sir, I cannot help expressing a wish that every member of the convention who may still have objections to it would with me on this occasion doubt a little of his own infallibility, and, to make *manifest* our *unanimity*, put his name to this instrument.

To Mrs. Jane Mecum.—
Philadelphia, 26 Nov., 1788.

I have long been accustomed to receive more blame, as well as more praise, than I have deserved. It is the lot of every public man, and I leave one account to balance the other.

PROSPECT FOR EMIGRANTS TO AMERICA.

No rewards are given to encourage new settlers to come among us, whatever degree of property they may bring with them, nor any exemptions from common duties. Our country offers to strangers nothing but a good climate, fertile soil, wholesome air, free government, wise laws, liberty, a good people to live among, and a hearty welcome. Those Europeans who have these or greater advantages at home, would do well to stay where they are.

THE ANCIENT JEWS AND THE ANTI-FEDERALISTS.

One would have thought that the appointment of men [Moses and Aaron] who had distinguished themselves in procuring the liberty of their nation, and had hazarded their lives in openly opposing the will of a powerful monarch who would have retained that nation in slavery, might have been an appointment acceptable to a grateful people ; and that a constitution framed for them by the Deity himself, might on that account have been secure of a universally welcome reception. Yet there were, in every one of the thirteen tribes, some discontented, restless spirits, who were continually exciting them to reject the proposed new government. . . .

I beg I may not be understood to infer, that our general convention was divinely inspired when it formed the new federal constitution, merely because that constitution has been unreasonably and violently opposed; yet I must own I have so much faith in the general government of the world by Providence that I can hardly conceive a transaction of such momentous importance to the welfare of millions now existing and to exist in the posterity of a great nation, should be suffered to pass without being in some degree influenced, guided and governed by that omnipotent, omnipresent and beneficent Ruler in whom all inferior spirits live, move and have their being.

To Samuel Moore.—
Philadelphia, 5 Nov., 1789.
I hope the fire of liberty, which you mention as spreading itself over Europe, will act

upon the inestimable rights of man, as common fire does upon gold ; purify without destroying them ; so that a lover of liberty may find a *country* in any part of Christendom.

ON THE ABOLITION OF SLAVERY.—

9 November, 1789.

Slavery is such an atrocious debasement of human nature, that its very extirpation, if not performed with solicitous care, may sometimes open a source of serious evils.

TO M. LEROY.—

Philadelphia, Nov. 13, 1789.

Our new Constitution is now established, and has an appearance that promises permanency ; but in this world nothing can be said to be certain, except death and taxes.

GEORGE WASHINGTON.

" Illustrious man! deriving honor less from the splendor of his situation than from the dignity of his mind ; before whom all borrowed greatness sinks into insignificance."—CHARLES JAMES FOX, *in the British Parliament.*

TO GEORGE WILLIAM FAIRFAX, in England. May 31, 1775.

The once happy and peaceful plains of America are either to be drenched with blood or inhabited by slaves. Sad alternative! But can a virtuous man hesitate in his choice?

TO THE PRESIDENT OF THE CONGRESS, upon his appointment as Commander-in-Chief. June 16, 1775.

Mr. President :—Though I am truly sensible of the high honor done me in this appointment, yet I feel great distress from a consciousness that my abilities and military experience may not be equal to the extensive and important trust. However, as the Congress desire it, I will enter upon the momentous duty and exert every power I possess in their service, for the support of the glorious cause. . . . As to pay, Sir, I beg leave to assure the Congress that as no pecuniary consideration could have tempted me to accept this arduous employment at the expense of my domestic ease and happiness, I do not wish to make any profit from it.   I will keep an exact account of my expenses.   Those I doubt not they will discharge, and that is all I desire.

FIRST ORDER TO CONTINENTAL ARMY.

July 4, 1775.

It is hoped that all distinctions of Colonies will be laid aside ; so that one and the same spirit may animate the whole, and the only contest be, who shall render, on this great and trying occasion, the most essential service to the great and common cause in which we are all engaged.

ARMY ORDER: PROHIBITION OF GAMING. 1776.

At this time of public distress, men may have enough to do in the service of God and their country, without abandoning themselves to vice and immorality. It is a noble cause in which we are engaged : it is the cause of virtue and mankind ; every advantage and comfort to us and our posterity depend upon the vigor of our exertions ; in short Freedom or Slavery must be the result of our conduct ; there can, therefore, be no greater inducement to men to behave well.

ARMY ORDER.

July 31, 1776.

It is with great concern, the General understands that Jealousies, etc., are arisen among the troops from the different Provinces, . . . The General most earnestly entreats the officers and soldiers to consider, . . . that all distinctions are sunk in the name of an American. To make this name honorable, and to preserve the liberty of our Country, ought to be our only emulation, and he will be the best Soldier and the best Patriot, who contributes most to this glorious work, whatsoever be his station, or from whatsoever part of the Continent, he may come.

To the Congress. 1777.

I find they [the Congress] have done me the honor to intrust me with powers in my military capacity, of the highest nature and almost unlimited in extent. Instead of thinking myself freed from all civil obligations, by this mark of their confidence, I shall constantly bear in mind, that as the sword was the last resort for the preservation of our liberties, so it ought to be the first thing laid aside, when those liberties are firmly established.

To the President of the Congress. Winter of Valley Forge. Dec. 23, 1777.

I can assure those gentlemen [the Pennsylvania Assembly], that it is a much easier and less distressing thing, to draw remonstrances in a comfortable room by a good fireside, than to occupy a cold, bleak hill and sleep under frost and snow, without clothes or blankets. However, although they seem to have little feeling for the naked and distressed soldiers, I feel superabundantly for them, and, from my soul, I pity those miseries, which it is neither in my power to relieve or prevent.

It is for these reasons, therefore, that I have dwelt upon this subject ; and it adds not a little to my other difficulties and distress, to find, that much more is expected from me than is possible to be performed, and that upon the ground of safety and policy I am obliged to conceal the true state of the army from public view, and thereby expose myself to detraction and calumny.

LETTER TO HIS AGENT, LUND WASHINGTON, who had saved Mt. Vernon from destruction at the hands of the British, by furnishing them supplies. April 30, 1781.

It would have been a less painful circumstance to me to have heard, that in consequence of your non-compliance with their

request, they have burned my House and laid
the Plantation in ruins. You ought to have
considered yourself as my representative,
and should have reflected on the bad example of communicating with the enemy,
and making a voluntary offer of refresh-
ments to them with a view to prevent conflagration.

REPLY TO COL. LEWIS NICOLA, proposing
    that Washington should make himself
    King.   May 22, 1782.

With a mixture of great surprise and
astonishment, I have read with attention
the sentiments you have submitted to my
perusal. Be assured, Sir, no occurrence in
the course of the war has given me more
painful sensations, than your information of
there being such ideas existing in the army,
as you have expressed, and I must view with
abhorrence and reprehend with severity. ....
Let me conjure you, then, if you have any
regard for your Country, concern for yourself or posterity, or respect for me, to banish
these thoughts from your mind, and never

communicate, as from yourself or any one else, a sentiment of the like nature.

To the Governors of All the States.
June 8, 1783.

The citizens of America, placed in the most enviable condition, as the sole lords and proprietors of a vast tract of continent, comprehending all the various soils and climates of the world, and abounding with all the necessaries and conveniences of life, are now, by the late satisfactory pacification, acknowledged to be possessed of absolute freedom and independency. They are, from this period, to be considered as the actors on a most conspicuous theatre, which seems to be peculiarly designated by Providence for the display of human greatness and felicity.

The foundation of our empire was not laid in the gloomy age of ignorance and superstition : but at an epocha when the rights of mankind were better understood and more clearly defined, than at any former period.

There are four things, which, I humbly
conceive, are essential to the well-being, I
may even venture to say, to the existence of
the United States, as an independent power.

First.   An indissoluble union of the States
under one federal head.

Secondly.   A sacred regard to public
justice.

Thirdly.   The adoption of a proper peace
establishment [of military defence] : and

Fourthly.   The prevalence of that pacific
and friendly disposition among the people
of the United States, which will induce them
to forget their local prejudices and policies ;
to make those mutual concessions, which
are requisite to the general prosperity ; and,
in some instances, to sacrifice their individual advantages to the interest of the community.

These are the pillars on which the glorious
fabric of our independency and national
character must be supported.   Liberty is the
basis ; and whoever would dare to sap the
foundation, or overturn the structure, under
whatever specious pretext he may attempt

it, will merit the bitterest execration, and the severest punishment which can be inflicted by his injured country.

It is indispensable to the happiness of the individual States, that there should be lodged somewhere a supreme power to regulate and govern the general concerns of the confederated republic, without which the Union cannot be of long duration.

Whatever measures have a tendency to dissolve the Union, or contribute to violate or lessen the sovereign authority, ought to be considered as hostile to the liberty and independency of America and the authors of them treated accordingly.

In this state of absolute freedom and perfect security, who will grudge to yield a very little of his property to support the common interest of society, and insure the protection of government?. . . . Where is the man to be found, who wishes to remain indebted for the defence of his own person and property, to the exertions, the bravery, and the

blood of others, without making one generous effort to repay the debt of honor and
gratitude? In what part of the continent
shall we find any man, or body of men, who
would not blush to stand up and propose
measures, purposely calculated to rob the
soldier of his stipend, and the public creditor
of his due?

The militia of this country must be considered as the palladium of our security, and
the first effectual resort in case of hostil-
ity. It is essential, therefore, that the same
system should pervade the whole ; that the
formation and discipline of the militia of the
Continent should be absolutely uniform, and
that the same species of arms, accouter-
ments, and military apparatus should be introduced in every part of the United States.
No one, who has not learned it from experience, can conceive the difficulty, expense,
and confusion, which result from a contrary
system, or the vague arrangements which
have hitherto prevailed.

FIRST INAUGURAL ADDRESS.
April 30, 1789.

No people can be bound to acknowledge and adore the invisible hand, which conducts the affairs of men, more than the people of the United States. Every step, by which they have advanced to the character of an independent Nation, seems to have been distinguished by some token of providential agency. And, in the important revolution just accomplished in the system of their united government, the tranquil deliberations and voluntary consent of so many distinct communities, from which the event has resulted, cannot be compared with the means by which most governments have been established, without some return of pious gratitude along with an humble anticipation of the future blessings which the past seem to presage.

There is no truth more thoroughly established, than that there exists in the economy and course of nature an indissoluble union between virtue and happiness, between duty and advantage, between the genuine maxims of an honest and magnanimous policy, and the solid rewards of public prosperity and felicity; since we ought to be no less persuaded that the propitious smiles of Heaven can never be expected on a nation that disregards the eternal rules of order and right, which Heaven itself has ordained; and since the preservation of the sacred fire of liberty, and the destiny of the republican model of government, are justly considered as *deeply*, perhaps as *finally* staked, on the experiment intrusted to the hands of the American people,

To Dr. David Stuart.

June, 1790.

If there was the same propensity in mankind for investigating the motives, as there is for censuring the conduct of public characters, it would be found, that the censure so freely bestowed, is oftentimes unmerited and uncharitable.

To Dr. David Stuart.

June, 1790.

That there is a diversity of interests in the Union, none has denied. That this is the case also in every State, is equally certain; and that it even extends to the counties of individual States, can be readily proved. . . . To constitute a dispute there must be two parties. To understand it well both parties, and all the circumstances, must be fully heard; and to accommodate differences, temper and mutual forbearance are requisite. Common danger brought the States into confederacy, and on their union our safety and importance depend. A spirit of accommodation was the basis of the present Constitution.

First Annual Address to Congress.

January 8, 1790.

Among the many interesting objects, which will engage your attention, that of providing for the common defence will merit particular regard. To be prepared for war is one of the most effectual means of preserving peace.

A free people ought not only to be armed, but disciplined ; to which end a uniform and well-designated plan is requisite.

TO HIS AGENT.
November, 1790.

I had rather have heard, that my repaired coach was plain and elegant than rich and elegant.

SECOND ANNUAL ADDRESS TO CONGRESS.
December 8, 1790.

To the House of Representatives :

Allow me, moreover, to hope that it will be a favorite policy with you, not merely to secure a payment of the interest of the debt funded, but as far and as fast as the growing resources of the country will permit, to exonerate it of the principal itself. The appropriations you have made of the western lands explain your disposition on this subject, and I am persuaded that the sooner that valuable fund can be made to contribute, along with other means, to the actual reduction of the public debt, the more salutary will the measure be to every public interest, as well as the most satisfactory to our constituents.

THIRD ANNUAL ADDRESS TO CONGRESS.
October 25, 1791.

It is sincerely to be desired that all need of coercion in future may cease; and that an intimate intercourse may succeed, calculated to advance the happiness of the Indians and to attach them firmly to the United States. . . . A system corresponding with the mild principles of religion and philanthropy toward an unenlightened race of men, whose happiness materially depends on the conduct of the United States, would be as honorable to the national character as conformable to the dictates of sound policy.

FIFTH ANNUAL ADDRESS TO CONGRESS.
December, 1793.

The United States ought not to indulge a persuasion that, contrary to the order of human events, they will forever keep at a distance those painful appeals to arms, with which the history of every other nation abounds. There is a rank due to the United States among nations which will be withheld, if not absolutely lost, by the reputation of weakness. If we desire to avoid insult, we must be able to repel it ; if we desire to secure peace, one of the most powerful instruments of our rising prosperity, it must be known that we are at all times ready for war.

No pecuniary consideration is more urgent than the regular redemption and discharge of the public debt. On none can delay be more injurious, or an economy of time more valuable.

SIXTH ANNUAL ADDRESS TO CONGRESS.
Nov. 19, 1794.

While there is a cause to lament, that occurrences of this nature [the Whiskey Rebellion in Pennsylvania] should have disgraced the name, or interrupted the tranquillity of any part of our community, or should have diverted to a new application any portion of the public resources, there are not wanting real and substantial consolations for the misfortune. It has demonstrated that our prosperity rests on solid foundations; by furnishing an additional proof that my fellow-citizens understand the true principles of government and liberty; that they feel their inseparable union; that, notwithstanding all the devices, which have been used to sway them from their interest and duty, they are now as ready to maintain the authority of the laws against licentious invasions as they were to defend their rights against usurpation.

It has been a spectacle displaying to the highest advantage the value of republican government, to behold the most and the least wealthy of our citizens standing in the same ranks as private soldiers; pre-eminently distinguished by being the army of the constitution; undeterred by a march of three hundred miles over rugged mountains, by the approach of an unclement season, or by any other discouragement.

SEVENTH ANNUAL ADDRESS TO CON-
GRESS. December, 1795.

With burthens so light as scarcely to be
perceived, with resources fully adequate to
our present exigencies, with governments
founded on the geniune principles of rational
liberty, and with mild and wholesome laws,
is it too much to say that our country exhib-
its a spectacle of national happiness never
surpassed, if ever before equalled ?

To inforce upon the Indians the observance of justice, it is indispensable that there
shall be competent means of rendering
justice to them.

FAREWELL ADDRESS TO THE PEOPLE OF
THE UNITED STATES. [Withdrawing
himself as a Candidate for the Presi-
dency.]

September 19, 1796.

Satisfied, that, if any circumstances have
given peculiar value to my services, they were
temporary, I have the consolation to believe,
that, while choice and prudence invite me to

quit the political scene, patriotism does not forbid it.

It is of infinite moment, that you should properly estimate the immense value of your national Union to your collective and individual happiness ;—that you should cherish a cordial, habitual, and immovable attachment to it : accustoming yourselves to think and speak of it as of the Palladium of your political safety and prosperity; watching for its preservation with jealous anxiety ; discountenancing whatever may suggest even a suspicion that it can in any event be abandoned; and indignantly frowning upon the first dawning of every attempt to alienate any portion of our Country from the rest, or to enfeeble the sacred ties which now link together the various parts.

The name of AMERICAN, which belongs to you, in your national capacity, must always exalt just pride of Patriotism, more than any appellation derived from local discriminations.

While, then, every part of our country thus feels an immediate and peculiar interest in Union, all the parts combined in the united mass of means and efforts cannot fail to find greater strength, greater resource, proportionably greater security from external danger, a less frequent interruption of their peace by foreign nations; . . . Hence, likewise, they will avoid the necessity of those overgrown military establishments, which, under any form of government, are inauspicious to liberty, and which are to be regarded as particularly hostile to republican Liberty.

Is there a doubt, whether a common government can embrace so large a sphere ? —Let experience solve it. . . . We are authorized to hope, that a proper organization of the whole, with the auxiliary agency of governments for the respective subdivisions, will afford a happy issue to the experiment.

This Government, the offspring of our

own choice uninfluenced and unawed, adopted upon full investigation and mature deliberation, completely free in its principles, in the distribution of its powers, uniting security with energy, and containing within itself a provision for its own amendment, has a just claim to your confidence and your support.

The basis of our political systems is the right of the people to make and to alter their Constitutions of Government.—But the Constitution which at any time exists, till changed by an explicit and authentic act of the whole people, is sacredly obligatory upon all.—The very idea of the power and right of the people to establish Government presupposes the duty of every individual to obey the established Government.

All obstructions to the execution of the Laws, all combinations and associations, under whatever plausible character, with the real design to direct, control, counteract, or awe the regular deliberation and action of the constituted authorities, are destructive of this fundamental principle, and of fatal tendency.

I have already intimated to you the danger of Parties in the State, with particular reference to the founding of them on Geographical discriminations.—Let me now take a more comprehensive view, and warn you in the most solemn manner against the baneful effects of the Spirit of Party, generally.

This Spirit, unfortunately, is inseparable from our nature, having its root in the strongest passions of the human mind.—It exists under different shapes in all Governments, more or less stifled, controlled, or repressed : but, in those of the popular form, it is seen in its greatest rankness, and is truly their worst enemy. . . . It serves always to distract the Public Councils, and enfeeble the Public Admistration.

There is an opinion, that parties in free countries are useful checks upon the Administration of the Government, and serve to keep alive the spirit of Liberty.—This within certain limits is probably true ; . . . From their natural tendency, it is certain there will always be enough of that spirit for every salutary purpose,—and there being constant danger of excess, the effort ought to be, by force of public opinion, to mitigate and assuage it.—A fire not to be quenched ; it demands a uniform vigilance to prevent its bursting into flame, lest, instead of warming, it should consume.

It is important, likewise, that the habits of thinking in a free country should inspire caution in those intrusted with its administration, to confine themselves within their respective constitutional spheres, avoiding in the exercise of the powers of one department to encroach upon another. . . . If, in the opinion of the People, the distribution of the modification of the Constitutional powers be in any particular wrong, let it be corrected by an amendment, in the way which the Constitution designates.—But let there be no change by usurpation ; for though this, in one instance, may be the instrument of good, it is the customary weapon by which free governments are destroyed.

Promote, then, as an object of primary importance, institutions for the general diffusion of knowledge.　In proportion as the structure of a government gives force to public opinion, it is essential that public opinion should be enlightened.

Observe good faith and justice towards all Nations ; cultivate peace and harmony with all.

Nothing is more essential, than that permanent, inveterate antipathies against particular nations, and passionate attachment for others, should　be　excluded ; and　that in place　of　them　just　and　amicable　feelings towards all should be cultivated.　The nation, which indulges towards another habitual hatred, or an　habitual fondness, is in some degree a slave.　It is a slave to its animosity or its affection, either of which is sufficient to lead it astray from its duty and its interest.

The great rule of conduct for us, in regard to foreign nations, is, in extending our commercial relations, to have with them as little *political* connection as possible.

Europe has a set of primary interests, which to us have none, or a very remote relation.—Hence she must be engaged in frequent controversies, the causes of which are essentially foreign to our concerns. . . . Our detached and distant situation invites and enables us to pursue a different course. . . . Why forego the advantages of so peculiar a situation ?—Why quit our own to stand upon foreign ground ?—Why, by interweaving our destiny with that of any part of Europe, entangle our peace and prosperity in the toils of European ambition, rivalship, interest, humor, or caprice ?

'Tis our true policy to steer clear of permanent alliances, with any portion of the foreign world. . . . Taking care always to keep ourselves, by suitable establishments on a respectably defensive posture, we may safely trust to temporary alliances for extraordinary emergencies.

Harmony, and a liberal intercourse with all nations, are recommended by policy, humanity, and interest. But even our commercial policy should hold an equal and impartial hand ; neither seeking nor granting exclusive favors or preferences ; . . . . constantly keeping in view, that 'tis folly in one nation to look for disinterested favors from another,—that it must pay with a portion of its independence for whatever it may accept under that character.

In offering to you, my Countrymen, these counsels of an old and affectionate friend, I dare not hope they will make the strong and lasting impression I could wish ; . . . . But, if I may even flatter myself, that they may be productive of some partial benefit ; some occasional good ; that they may now and then recur to moderate the fury of party spirit, to warn against the mischiefs of foreign intrigue, to guard against the impostures of pretended patriotism, this hope will be a full recompense for the solicitude for your welfare, by which they have been dictated.

EIGHTH ANNUAL ADDRESS TO CONGRESS.
December 7, 1796.

To an active external commerce, the protection of a naval force is indispensable. This is manifest with regard to wars, in which a state itself is a party. But besides this, it is in our own experience, that the most sincere neutrality is not a sufficient guard against the depredations of nations at war. To secure respect to a neutral flag requires a naval force, organized and ready to vindicate it from insult or aggression. This may even prevent the necessity of going to war, by discouraging belligerent powers from committing such violations of the rights of the neutral party, as may, first or last, leave no other option.

It will not be doubted, that, with reference either to individual or national welfare, agriculture is of primary importance. In proportion as nations advance in population and other circumstances of maturity, this truth becomes more apparent.

A primary object of such a national institution [University] should be the education of our youth in the science of *government*. In a republic, what species of knowledge can be equally important? and what duty more pressing on its legislature than to patronize a plan for communicating it to those who are to be the future guardians of the liberties of the country?

The institution of a military academy is also recommended by cogent reasons. However pacific the general policy of a nation be, it ought never to be without an adequate stock of military knowledge for emergencies. The first would impair the energy of its character, and both would hazard its safety or expose it to greater evils when war could not be avoided—besides, that war might often not depend upon its own choice.

In proportion as the observance of pacific

maxims might exempt a nation from the necessity of practising the rules of military art, ought to be its care in preserving and transmitting, by proper establishments, the knowledge of that art. Whatever argument may be drawn from particular examples, superficially viewed, a thorough examination of the subject will evince that the art of war is at once comprehensive and complicated, that it demands much previous study ; and that the possession of it, in its most improved and perfect state, is always of great moment to the security of a nation.

The compensation to the officers of the United States, in various instances, and in none more than in respect to the most important stations, appear to call for legislative revision. The consequences of a defective provision are of serious import to the government. If private wealth is to supply the defect of public retribution, it will greatly contract the sphere within which the selection of character for office is to be made, and will proportionally diminish the probability of a choice of men able as well as upright. Besides that, it would be repugnant to the vital principles of our government, virtually to exclude from public trusts talents and virtue unless accompanied by wealth.

It will afford me a heartfelt satisfaction to concur in such further measures as will ascertain to our country the prospect of a speedy extinguishment of the [public] debt. Posterity may have cause to regret if from any motive intervals of tranquillity are left unimproved for accelerating this valuable end.

The situation in which I now stand, for the last time, in the midst of the representatives of the people of the United States, naturally recalls the period when the administration of the present form of government commenced ; and I cannot omit the occasion to congratulate you and my country on the success of the experiment, nor to repeat my fervent supplications to the Supreme Ruler of the Universe and Sovereign Arbiter of Nations that his providential care may still be extended to the United States; that the virtue and happiness of the people may be preserved; and that the government, which they have instituted for the protection of their liberties, may be perpetual.

MISCELLANEA.

Of all dispositions and habits which lead to political prosperity, religion and morality are indispensable supports. In vain would that man claim the tribute of Patriotism, who should labor to subvert these great pillars of human-happiness, these firmest props of the duties of men and citizens. The mere politician, equally with the pious man, ought to respect and cherish them.

Every nation has a right to establish that form of government under which it conceives it may live most happy; provided it infracts no right, or is not dangerous to others; and no governments ought to interfere with the internal concerns of another, except for the security of what is due to themselves.

To the efficacy and permanency of the Union, a Government for the whole is indispensable. No *alliances*, however strict, between the parts, can be an adequate substitute ; they must inevitably experience the infractions and interruptions, which all alliances in all times have experienced.

The very idea of the power and the right of the people to establish government, presupposes the duty of every individual to obey the established government.

In every nomination to office, I have endeavored, as far as my own knowledge extended, or information could be obtained, to make fitness of character my primary object.

America may think herself happy in having the Atlantic for a barrier.

Let us, as a nation, be just ; let us fulfill the public contracts, which Congress had undoubtedly a right to make, with the same good faith we suppose ourselves bound to perform our private engagements.

Commerce and industry are the best mines of the nation.

A difference of opinion on political points is not to be imputed to freemen as a fault. It is to be presumed, that they are all actuated by an equally laudable and sacred regard for the liberties of their country.

Arms should be the last resort.

THOMAS JEFFERSON.

" All honor to Jefferson ; to the man who, in the con-
crete pressure of a struggle for national independence
by a single people, had the coolness, forecast and capacity to introduce into a merely revolutionary document an abstract truth, applicable to all men and all
times, and so to embalm it there that to-day, and in all
coming days, it shall be a rebuke and a stumbling-block
to the harbingers of reappearing tyranny and oppression."—ABRAHAM LINCOLN.

AUTOBIOGRAPHY.

In 1769, I became a member of the legislature [of Virginia] by the choice of the
county in which I live, and so continued
until it was closed by the Revolution. I
made one effort in that body for the permis-
sion of the emancipation of slaves, which
was rejected ; and, indeed, during the regal
government, nothing liberal could expect
success. Our minds were circumscribed
within narrow limits, by an habitual belief
that it was our duty to be subordinate to the
mother country in all matters of govern-

ment, to direct all our labors in subservience to her interests, and even to observe a bigoted intolerance for all religions but hers.

The difficulties with our representatives were of habit and despair, not of reflection and conviction. Experience soon proved that they could bring their minds to rights, on the first summons of their attention.

AUTOBIOGRAPHY.

Being elected one for my own county [to the preliminary Convention, 1774], I prepared a draught of instructions to be given to the delegates whom we should send to the [First Continental] Congress, and which I meant to propose at our meeting. In this I took the ground which, from the beginning I had thought the only one orthodox or tenable, which was that the relation between Great Britain and these Colonies was exactly the same as that of England and Scotland, after the accession of James, and until the Union, and the same as her present relations with Hanover, having the same Executive chief but no other necessary political connection ; and that our emigration from England to this country gave her no more rights over us, than the emigration of the Danes and Saxons gave to the present authorities of the mother country, over England. . . . .expatriation being a natural right, and acted on as such, by all nations, in all ages.

To John Randolph.
Monticello, August 25, 1775.

I . . . . would rather be in dependence on Great Britain, properly limited, than on any other nation on earth, or than on no nation. But I am one of those, too, who, rather than submit to the rights of legislation for us, assumed by the British Parliament, and which late experience has shown they will so cruelly exercise, would lend my hand to sink the whole Island in the ocean.

To John Randolph.
November, 1775.

Believe me, dear sir, there is not in the British empire a man who more cordially

loves a union with Great Britain than I do.
But by the God that made me, I will cease
to exist before I yield to a connection on such
terms as the British Parliament propose ; and
in this, I think I speak the sentiments of
America.   We want neither inducement nor
power, to declare and assert a separation.
It is will, alone, which is wanting, and that
is growing apace under the fostering hand
of our king.

DECLARATION OF INDEPENDENCE [The
   Slave Trade—One of the Charges
   against the King, Which Was Omitted
   by Congress].   1776.

He has waged cruel war against human
nature itself, violating its most sacred rights
of life and liberty in the persons of a distant people who never offended him, capti-
vating and carrying them into slavery in
another hemisphere, or to incur miserable
death in their transportation thither.   This
piratical welfare, the opprobrium of infidel
powers, is the warfare of the Christian King
of Great Britain.   Determined to keep open

a market where men should be bought and sold, he has prostituted his negative for suppressing every legislative attempt to prohibit or to restrain this execrable commerce.

DECLARATION OF INDEPENDENCE.

4 July, 1776.

We hold these truths to be self-evident ; that all men are created equal ; that they are endowed by their creator with certain inalienable rights ; that among these are life, liberty, and the pursuit of happiness ; that to secure these rights, governments are instituted among men, deriving their just powers from the consent of the governed ; that, whenever any form of government becomes destructive of these ends, it is the right of the people to alter or abolish it, and to institute a new government, laying its foundations on such principles, and organizing its powers in such form, as to them shall seem most likely to effect their safety and happiness. . . .

Mankind are more disposed to suffer, while evils are sufferable, than to right themselves by abolishing the forms to which they are accustomed. But when a long train of abuses and usurpations, pursuing invariably the same object, evinces a design to reduce them under absolute despotism, it is their right, it is their duty, to throw off such government, and to provide new guards for their security.

We, therefore, the representatives of the United States of America, in general Congress assembled, appealing to the supreme judge of the world for the rectitude of our intentions, do, in the name, and by the authority of the good people of these Colonies, solemnly publish and declare that these United Colonies are, and of right ought to be *free and independent States*; . . . . And for the support of this declaration, with a firm reliance on the protection of divine providence, we mutually pledge to each other our lives, our fortunes, and our sacred honor.

AUTOBIOGRAPHY.

If the present Congress [1783] errs in too much talking how can it be otherwise, in a body to which the people send one hundred and fifty lawyers, whose trade it is to question every thing, yield nothing, and talk by the hour? That one hundred and fifty lawyers should do business together, ought not to be expected.

ORDINANCE OF 1784. For the Government of New Territories.

Resolved, That the territory ceded by individual States to the United States, whensoever the same shall have been purchased of the Indian inhabitants and offered for sale by the United States, shall be formed into additional States. . . . provided, That both the temporary and permanent governments be established on these principles as their basis :

1. That they shall forever remain a part of the United States of America. . . .

5. That after the year 1800 of the Christian era there shall be neither slavery nor involuntary servitude in any of the said States, otherwise than in punishment of crimes, whereof the party shall have been duly convicted to have been personally guilty. [This Anti-sla-

very provision killed the bill at that time.
It was included in the Permanent " Ordinance of 1787," with the addition, however,
of a Fugitive Slave provision.]

To J. Banister.
Paris, 1785.

It appears to me, then, that an American,
coming to Europe for education, loses in
his knowledge, in his morals, in his health,
in his habits, and in his happiness.

To a Friend.
Paris, January 25, 1786.

Our present federal limits are not too
large for good government, nor will the increase of votes in the Congress produce any
ill effect.   On the contrary, it will drown the
little divisions at present existing there.
Our Confederacy must be viewed as the
nest, from which all America, North and
South, is to be peopled.

To James Monroe.
August 11, 1786.

A naval force can never endanger our

liberties, nor occasion bloodshed ; a land force would do both.

To Edward Carrington.
Paris, January 16, 1787.

The basis of our governments being the opinion of the people, the very first object should be to keep that right; and were it left to me to decide whether we should have a government without newspapers or newspapers without a government, I should not hesitate a moment to prefer the latter. But I should mean that every man should receive those papers and be capable of reading them.

To George Wythe.
Paris, August 13, 1787.

If all the sovereigns of Europe were to set themselves to work to emancipate the minds of their subjects from their present ignorance and prejudices, and that as zealously as they now endeavor the contrary, a thousand years would not place them on that high ground, on which our common people are now setting out. Ours could not have been so fairly put into the hands of their own common sense, had they not been separated from their parent stock and kept from contamination, either from them, or the other people of the old world, by the intervention of so wide an ocean. To know the worth of this, one must see the want of it here. I think by far the most important bill in our whole code is that for the diffusion of knowledge among the people. No other sure foundation can be devised, for the preservation of freedom and happiness.

If anybody thinks that kings, nobles, or priests are good conservators of the public happiness, send him here. It is the best school in the universe to cure him of that folly. He will see here with his own eyes, that these descriptions of men are an abandoned confederacy against the happiness of the mass of the people. Preach, my dear sir, a crusade against ignorance; establish and improve the law for educating the common people.

To His Daughter.

March, 1787.

It is part of the American character to consider nothing as desperate, to surmount every difficulty by resolution and contrivance. Remote from all other aid, we are obliged to invent and to execute ; to find means within ourselves, and not to lean on others.

To General Washington.

Paris, 1788.

I was much an enemy to monarchy before I came to Europe. I am ten thousand times more so, since I have seen what they are. There is scarcely an evil known in these countries, which may not be traced to their king as its source, nor a good which is not derived from the small fibers of republicanism existing among them. I can further say with safety there is not a crowned head in Europe, whose talents or merit would entitle him to be elected a vestryman by the people of any parish in America.

To David Humphreys.

March 18, 1789.

Whenever our affairs go obviously wrong the good sense of the people will interpose, ' and set them to rights. The example of changing a constitution, by assembling the wise men of the State, instead of assembling armies, will be worth as much to the world as the former examples we had given them.

To James Madison.

Paris, August 28, 1789.

I know of but one code of morality for men, whether acting singly or collectively. He who says I will be a rogue when I act in company with a hundred others but an honest man when I act alone, will be believed in the former assertion, but not in the latter.

To Mr. Madison.

Paris, September 6, 1789.

No society can make a perpetual constitution, or even perpetual law. The earth belongs always to the living generation. They may manage it then, and what proceeds from it, as they please, during their usufruct.

To the Mayor of Alexandria, Va.
March 11, 1790.

It is indeed an animating thought that, while we are securing the rights of ourselves and our posterity, we are pointing out the way to struggling nations who wish, like us, to emerge from their tyrannies also. Heaven help their struggle, and lead them, as it has done us, triumphantly through them.

To a Friend.
December 23, 1791.

I would rather be exposed to the inconveniences attending too much liberty, than those attending too small a degree of it.

Report on Convention with Spain.
March 22, 1792.

Most codes extend their definitions of treason to acts not really against one's country. They do not distinguish between acts against the *Government* and acts against the

Oppressions of the Government. The latter are virtues : yet have furnished more victims to the Executioner than the former. Because real Treasons are rare ; Oppressions frequent. The unsuccessful Struggles against Tyranny have been the chief Martyrs of Treason laws in all countries. . . . We should not wish, then, to give up to the Executioner, the Patriot who fails and flees to us. Treasons, then, taking the *simulated* with the *real*, are sufficiently punished by Exile.

To ELBRIDGE GERRY.
January 26, 1799.

I am for a government rigorously frugal and simple, applying all the possible savings of the public revenue to the discharge of the national debt ; and not for a multiplication of officers and salaries merely to make partisans, and for increasing, by every device, the public debt, on the principle of its being a public blessing.

I am for free commerce with all nations ;

political connection with none ; and little or no diplomatic establishment.

I am for freedom of religion, and against all maneuvers to bring about a legal ascendancy of one sect over another ; for freedom of the press, and against all violations of the Constitution to silence by force and not by reason the complaints or criticisms, just or unjust, of our citizens against the conduct of their agents.

And I am for encouraging the progress of science in all its branches ; and not for raising a hue and cry against the sacred name of philosophy ; for awing the human mind by stories of rawhead and bloody-bones to a distrust of its own vision, and to repose implicitly on that of others ; to go backwards instead of forwards to look for improvement ; to believe that government, religion, morality, and every other science were in the highest perfection in ages of the darkest ignorance ; and that nothing can ever be devised more perfect than what was established by our forefathers.

First Inaugural Address.

March 4, 1801.

All, too, will bear in mind this sacred principle, that though the will of the majority is to in all cases to prevail, that will, to be rightful, must be reasonable ; that the minority possess their equal rights, which equal laws must protect, and to violate would be oppression.

Every difference of opinion is not a difference of principle. We have called, by different names, brethren of the same principles. We are all republicans, we are all federalists. If there be any among us who would wish to dissolve this Union, or to change its republican form, let them stand undisturbed, as monuments of the safety with which error of opinion may be tolerated where reason is left free to combat it.

I know, indeed, that some honest men have feared that a republican government cannot be strong ; . . . . I believe this, on the contrary the strongest government on earth. I believe it is the only one where every man, at the call of the law, would fly to the standard of the law; would meet invasions of public order as his own personal concern.

Sometimes it is said that Man cannot be trusted with the government of himself. Can he, then, be trusted with the government of others? Or have we found angels in the forms of kings to govern him? Let History answer this question.

A wise and frugal government, which shall restrain men from injuring one another, shall leave them otherwise free to regulate their own pursuits of industry and improvement, and shall not take from the mouth of labor the bread it has earned; this is the sum of good government, and this is necessary to close the circle of our felicities.

Equal and exact justice to all men, of whatever state and persuasion, religious or political: Peace, commerce, and honest friendship with all nations, entangling alliances with none: The support of the State governments in all their rights, as the most competent administration for our domestic concerns and the surest bulwarks against anti-republican tendencies: The preservation of the General Government in its whole constitutional vigor, as the sheet-anchor of our peace at home and safety abroad : A jealous care of the right of election by the people, a mild and safe corrective of abuses, which are lopped by the sword of revolution where peaceable remedies are unprovided : Absolute acquiescence in the decisions of the majority, the vital principle of republics, from which there is no appeal but to force, the vital principle and immediate parent of despotism : A well-disciplined militia, our best reliance in peace and for the first moments of war, till regulars may relieve them : The supremacy of the civil over the military authority : Economy in public expense, that labor may be lightly burthened : The honest payment of our debts and sacred preservation of the public faith : Encouragement of agriculture, and of commerce as its hand-maid : The diffusion of information, and arraignment of all abuses at the bar of the public reason : Freedom of religion, freedom of the press, and freedom of person under the protection of the Habeas Corpus: and Trial by juries impartially selected.

These principles form the bright constellation which has gone before us, and guided our steps, through an age of Revolution and Reformation. . . .

They should be of the creed of our political faith, the text of civil instruction, the touchstone by which to try the services of those we trust ; and should we wander from them in moments of error or alarm, let us hasten to retrace our steps and regain the road which alone leads to peace, liberty and safety.

TO GEORGE JEFFERSON.
March 27, 1801.

The public will never be made to believe that the appointment of a relative is made on the ground of merit alone, uninfluenced by family views ; nor can they ever see, with approbation, offices, the disposal of which they intrusted to their Presidents for public purposes, divided out as family property. . . . It is true that this places the relations of a President in a worse situation than if he were a stranger, but the public good, which can not be affected if its confidence be lost, requires this sacrifice. Perhaps, too, it is compensated by sharing in the public esteem.

FIRST ANNUAL MESSAGE TO CONGRESS.
December 1, 1801.

One of the Tripolitan cruisers having fallen in with, and engaged the small schooner *Enterprise*, commanded by Lieutenant Sterret, which had gone as a tender to our larger vessels, was captured, after a heavy slaughter of her men, without the loss of a single one on our part. The bravery exhibited by our citizens on that element will, I trust, be a testimony to the world that it is not the want of that virtue which makes us seek their peace, but a conscientious desire to direct the energies of our nation to the multiplication of the human race, and not to its destruction.

Sound principles will not justify our taxing the industry of our fellow-citizens to accumulate treasure for wars to happen we know not when, and which might not perhaps happen but from the temptations offered by that treasure.

Agriculture, manufactures, commerce, and navigation, the four pillars of our prosperity, are the most thriving when left most free to individual enterprise.

SECOND MESSAGE TO CONGRESS.
December 12, 1802.

When effects so salutary result from the plans you have already sanctioned, when merely by avoiding false objects of expense we are able, without a direct tax, without internal taxes, and without borrowing, to make large and effectual payments toward the discharge of our public debt and the emancipation of our posterity from that moral canker, it is an encouragement, fellow-citizens, of the highest order, to proceed as we have begun, in substituting economy for taxation, and in pursuing what is useful for a nation placed as we are, rather than what is practised by others under different circumstances.

THIRD MESSAGE TO CONGRESS.
October 17, 1803.

We should be most unwise, indeed, were we to cast away the singular blessings of the position in which nature has placed us, the opportunity she has endowed us with of pursuing, at a distance from foreign contentions, the paths of industry, peace, and happiness ; of cultivating general friendship, and of bringing collisions of interest to the umpirage of reason rather than of force.

FOURTH MESSAGE TO CONGRESS.
November 8, 1804.

To those who expect us to calculate whether a compliance with unjust demands will not cost us less than a war, we must leave as a question of calculation for them, also, whether to retire from unjust demands will not cost them less than a war. We can do to each other very sensible injuries by war, but the mutual advantages of peace make that the best interest of both.

SECOND INAUGURAL ADDRESS.
March 4, 1805.

With nations, as with individuals, our interests soundly calculated, will ever be found inseparable from our moral duties : and history bears witness to the fact, that a just nation is trusted on its word, when resource is had to armaments and wars to bridle others.

SIXTH ANNUAL MESSAGE TO CONGRESS.
December 1, 1806.

Were armies to be raised whenever a speck of war is visible in our horizon, we never should have been without them. Our resources would have been exhausted on dangers which have never happened, instead of being reserved for what is really to take place.

TO SAMUEL KERCHIVAL.

July 12, 1816.

Some men look at constitutions with sanctimonious reverence, and deem them like the ark of the covenant, too sacred to be touched. They ascribe to the men of the preceding age a wisdom more than human, and suppose what they did to be beyond amendment. I knew that age well; I belonged to it, and labored with it. It deserved well of its country. It was very like the present, but without the experience of the present ; and forty years of experience in government is worth a century of book-reading ; and this they would say themselves, were they to rise from the dead. I am certainly not an advocate for frequent and untried changes in laws and constitutions. I think moderate imperfections had better be borne with ; because, when once known, we accommodate ourselves to them, and find practical means of correcting their ill effects. But I know also, that laws and institutions must go hand in hand with the progress of the human mind.

To a Friend.

I am not a Federalist, because I never submitted the whole system of my opinions to the creed of any party of men whatever, in religion, in philosophy, in politics, or in any thing else where I was capable of thinking for myself. Such an addiction is the last degradation of a free and moral agent. If I could not go to Heaven but with a party, I would not go there at all.

Autobiography.
Written in 1821.

The bill [in the Virginia Assembly 1779] on the subject of slavery was a mere digest of the existing laws. . . . the principles of the Amendment, however, were agreed on, that is to say, the freedom of all born after a certain day, and deportation after a certain age, but it was found that the public mind would not yet bear the proposition, nor will it bear it even at this day. Yet the day is not far distant when it must bear it, or worse will follow. Nothing is more cer-

tainly written in the book of fate than that
these people are to be free.

To President Monroe.
October 24, 1823.

Our first and fundamental maxim should
be, never to entangle ourselves in the broils
of Europe.

Our second, never to suffer Europe to
intermeddle with cis-Atlantic affairs.

America, North and South, has a set of
interests distinct from those of Europe, and
peculiarly her own. She should therefore
have a system of her own, separate and
apart from that of Europe.

To James Heaton.   Concerning the Abolition of Slavery.   May 26, 1826.

The revolution in public opinion which
this case requires, is not to be expected in a
day, or perhaps in an age ; but time, which
outlives all things, will outlive this evil also.
My sentiments have been forty years before
the public, and had I repeated them forty
times, they would only become the more

stale and threadbare. Although I shall not
live to see them consummated, they will not
die with me ; but, living or dying, they will
ever be in my most fervent prayers.

To Mr. Weightman.
Monticello, June 24, 1826.

I should, indeed, with peculiar delight,
have met and exchanged there congratula-
tions personally with the small band, the
remnant of that host of worthies, who joined
with us on that day [July 4, 1776], in the
bold and doubtful election we were to make
for our country, between submission or the
sword ; and to have enjoyed with them the
consolatory fact that our fellow citizens,
after half a century of experience and prosperity, continue to approve the choice we
made.

All eyes are opened or opening, to the
rights of man. The general spread of the
light of science has already laid open to
every view the palpable truth, that the mass
of mankind has not been born with saddles

on their backs, nor a favored few booted and spurred, ready to ride them legitimately, by the grace of God. These are grounds of hope for others. For ourselves, let the annual return of this day forever refresh our recollections of these rights, and our undiminished devotion to them.

DANIEL WEBSTER.

" He taught the principles of political Union to his
generation. He produced those convictions which
sustained the North in its subsequent contest to preserve the integrity of the Nation. There can be no
estimate of the services he rendered to the country by
his grand and patriotic efforts.''—Dr. John Lord.

It is certain, that, although many of them
were republicans in principle, we have no
evidence that our New England ancestors
would have emigrated, as they did, from
their own native country, would have become
wanderers in Europe, and finally would have
undertaken the establishment of a colony
here, merely from their dislike of the political systems of Europe. They fled not so
much from the civil government, as from
the hierarchy, and the laws which enforced
conformity to the church establishment. . . .
Thanks be to God, that this spot was honored
as the asylum of religious liberty! May its
standard, reared here, remain forever! May
it rise up as high as heaven, till its banner

shall fan the air of both continents, and wave as a glorious ensign of peace and security to the nations !

Whatever constitutes *country*, except the earth and the sun, all the moral causes of affection and attachment which operate upon the heart, they had brought with them to their new abode. Here were now their families and friends, their homes, and their property. Before they reached the shore, they had established the elements for a social system, and at a much earlier period had settled their forms of religious worship. . . . The morning that beamed on the first night of their repose saw the Pilgrims already *at home* in their country. There were political institutions, and civil liberty, and religious worship. Poetry has fancied nothing, in the wanderings of heroes, so distinct and characteristic.

Happy auspices of a happy futurity ! Who would wish that his country's existence had otherwise begun ? Who would desire the power of going back to the ages of fable ? ·

Who would wish for an origin obscured in the darkness of antiquity? Who would wish for other emblazoning of his country's heraldry, or other ornaments of her genealogy, than to be able to say, that her first existence was with intelligence, her first breath the inspiration of liberty, her first principle, the truth of divine religion?

Of our system of government the first thing to be said is, that it is really and practically a free system. It originates entirely with the people, and rests on no other foundation than their assent.

For the purpose of public instruction, we hold every man subject to taxation in proportion to his property, and we look not to the question, whether he himself have, or have not, children to be benefited by the education for which he pays. . . . We hope for a security beyond the law, and above the law, in the prevalence of an enlightened and well-principled and moral sentiment.

We are bound to maintain public liberty, and, by the example of our own systems, to convince the world that order and law, religion and morality, the rights of conscience, the rights of persons, and the rights of property, may all be preserved and secured, in the most perfect manner, by a government entirely and purely elective. If we fail in this, our disaster will be signal.

THE REVOLUTION IN GREECE.
January 19, 1824.

It is certainly true that the just policy of this country is, in the first place, a peaceful policy. No nation ever had less to expect from forcible aggrandizement. The mighty agents which are working out our greatness are time, industry, and the arts. Our augmentation is by growth, not by acquisition ; by internal development, not by external accession. No schemes can be suggested to us so magnificent as the prospects which a sober contemplation of our own condition, unaided by projects, uninfluenced by ambition, fairly spreads before us.

From the earliest settlement of these

states, their inhabitants were accustomed, in a greater or less degree, to the enjoyment of the powers of self-government; and for the last half-century they have sustained systems of government entirely representative, yielding to themselves the greatest possible prosperity, and not leaving them without distinction and respect among the nations of the earth. This system we are not likely to abandon; and while we shall no farther recommend its adoption to other nations, in whole or in part, than it may recommend itself by its visible influence on our own growth and prosperity, we are, nevertheless, interested to resist the establishment of doctrines which deny the legality of its foundations.

THE BUNKER HILL MONUMENT; LAYING THE CORNER STONE. June 17, 1825.

VENERABLE MEN! [1] You have come down to us from a former generation. Heaven has bounteously lengthened out your lives, that you might behold this joyous day. You are

---

[1] The veterans of 1775.

now where you stood fifty years ago, this very
hour, with your brothers and with your neigh-
bors, shoulder to shoulder, in the strife for
your country. Behold, how altered! The
same heavens are indeed over your heads : the
same ocean rolls at your feet ; but all else
how changed! You hear now no roar of
hostile cannon, you see no mixed volumes of
smoke and flame rising from burning
Charlestown. The ground strewed with the
dead and dying ; the impetuous charge ;
the steady and successful repulse ; the loud
call to repeated assault ; the summoning of all
that is manly to repeated resistance ; a thousand bosoms freely and fearlessly bared in
an instant to whatever of terror there may
be in war and death ;—all these you have
witnessed, but you witness them no more.
All is peace. The heights of yonder metrop-
olis, its towers and roofs, which you then
saw filled with wives and children and
countrymen in distress and terror, and look-
ing with unutterable emotions for the issue
of the combat, have presented you to-day
with the sight of its whole happy population,

come out to welcome and greet you with a universal jubilee. Yonder proud ships, by a felicity of position appropriately lying at the foot of this mount, and seeming fondly to cling around it, are not means of annoyance to you, but your country's own means of distinction and defence. All is peace ; and God has granted you this sight of your country's happiness, ere you slumber in the grave. He has allowed you to behold and to partake the reward of your patriotic toils, and he has allowed us, your sons and countrymen, to meet you here, and in the name of the present generation, in the name of your country, in the name of liberty, to thank you !

The great wheel of political revolution began to move in America. Here its rotation was guarded, regular and safe. Transferred to the other continent, from unfortunate but natural causes, it received an irregular and violent impulse ; it whirled along with a fearful celerity ; till at length, like the chariot-wheels in the races of antiquity, it took fire from the rapidity of its own motion, and blazed onward, spreading conflagration and terror around.

We learn from the result of this experiment, how fortunate was our own condition, and how admirably the character of our people was calculated for setting the great example of popular governments.

If, in our case, the representative system ultimately fail, popular governments must be pronounced impossible. No combination of circumstances more favorable to the experiment can ever be expected to occur. The last hopes of mankind therefore, rest with us ; and if it should be proclaimed, that our example had become an argument against the experiment, the knell of popular liberty would be sounded throughout the earth.

There remains to us a great duty of defence and preservation ; and there is opened to us, also, a noble pursuit, to which the spirit of the times strongly invites us. Our proper business is improvement. . . . Let our conceptions· be enlarged to the circle of our duties. Let us extend our ideas over the whole of the vast field in which we are called to act. Let our object be, OUR COUNTRY, OUR WHOLE COUNTRY, AND NOTHING BUT OUR COUNTRY. And, by the blessings of God, may that country itself become a vast, splendid monument, not of oppression and terror, but of Wisdom, of Peace, and of Liberty, upon which the world may gaze with admiration forever!

COMPLETION OF THE BUNKER HILL MONUMENT. June 7, 1843.

Heaven has not alloted to this generation an opportunity of rendering high services, and manifesting strong personal devotion, such as they rendered and manifested, and in such a cause as that which roused the patriotic fires of their youthful breasts, and nerved the strength of their arms. But we may praise what we cannot equal, and celebrate actions which we were not born to perform.

Some differences may, doubtless, be traced at this day between the descendants

of the early colonists of Virginia and those of
New England, owing to the different influences and different circumstances under
which the respective settlements were made ;
but only enough to create a pleasing variety
in the midst of a general family resem-
blance. . . . The great and common cause
of the Revolution bound them to one
another by new links of brotherhood ; and at
length the present constitution of government united them happily and gloriously, to
form the great republic of the world, and
bound up their interests and fortunes, till the
whole earth sees that there is now for them,
in present possession as well as in future
hope, but " ONE COUNTRY, ONE CONSTI-
TUTION, AND ONE DESTINY."

Spain descended on the New World in
the armed and terrible image of her monarchy and her soldiery ; England approached
it in the winning and popular garb of personal rights, public protection and civil
freedom. England transplanted liberty to
America ; Spain transplanted power. England, through the agency of private compan-

ies and the efforts of individuals, colonized this part of North America by industrious individuals, making their own way in the wilderness, defending themselves against the savages, recognizing their right to the soil, and with a general honest purpose of introducing knowledge as well as Christianity among them. Spain stooped on South America, like a vulture on its prey. Everything was force. Territories were acquired by fire and sword. Cities were destroyed by fire and sword. Hundreds of thousands of human beings fell by fire and sword. Even conversion to Christianity was attempted by fire and sword.

The great elements, then, of the American system of government, originally introduced by the colonists, and which were early in operation, and ready to be developed, more and more, as the progress of events should justify or demand, were,—

Escape from the existing political systems of Europe, including its religious hierarchies, but the continued possession and enjoyment of its science and arts, its literature, and its manners ;

Home government, or the power of making in the colony the municipal laws which were to govern it ;

Equality of rights ;

Representative assemblies, or forms of government founded on popular elections.

Let us hold fast the great truth, that communities are responsible as well as individuals ; that no government is respectable, which is not just ; that without unspotted purity of public faith, without sacred public principle, fidelity, and honor, no mere forms of government, no machinery of laws, can give dignity to political society.

THE MONROE DOCTRINE.

April 14, 1826.

We mean by our policy of neutrality, that the great objects of national pursuit with us are connected with peace. We covet no provinces ; we desire no conquests ; we entertain no ambitious projects of aggrandizement by war. This is our policy. But it does not follow from this, that we rely less than other nations on our own power to vindicate our own rights. We know that the last logic of kings is also our last logic ; that our own interests must be defended and maintained by our own arm ; and that peace or war may not always be of our own choosing.

I must now ask the indulgence of the committee to an important point in the discussion, I mean the declaration of the President in 1823.[1]

Sir, I look on the message of December, 1823, as forming a bright page in our history. I will help neither to erase it or tear it out ; nor shall it be, by any act of mine,

[1]In the message of President Monroe to Congress at the commencement of the session of 1823-24, the following passage occurs :— " In the wars of the European powers, in matters relating to themselves, we have never taken any part, nor does it comport with our policy so to do. It is only when our rights are invaded or seriously menaced, that we resent injuries or make preparations for defence. With the movements in this hemisphere we are of necessity more immediately connected, and by causes which must be obvious to all enlightened and impartial observers. . . . With the

blurred or blotted. It did honor to the sagacity of the government, and I will not diminish that honor. It elevated the hopes,
and gratified the patriotism, of the people.
Over those hopes I will not bring a mildew ;
nor will I put that gratified patriotism to
shame.

ADAMS AND JEFFERSON.

Aug. 2, 1826.

ADAMS AND JEFFERSON are no more. On
our fiftieth anniversary, the great day of
national jubilee, in the very hour of public
rejoicing, in the midst of echoing and re-echo-
ing voices of thanksgiving, while their own
names were on all tongues, they took their
flight together to the world of spirits.[1]

existing colonies or dependencies of any European
power, we have not interfered and shall not interfere.
But with the governments who have declared their
independence and maintained it, and whose independence we have on great consideration and on just
principles acknowledged, we could not view any inter-
position for the purpose of oppressing, or controll-
ing in any other manner their destiny, in any other
light than as the manifestation of an unfriendly disposition toward the United States.

[1] Both died July 4th, 1826.

ADAMS AND JEFFERSON are no more. As human beings, indeed, they are no more. .... But how little is there of the great and good which can die ! To their country they yet live, and live forever. They live in all that perpetuates the remembrance of men on earth ; in the reproofs of their own great actions, in the offspring of their intellect, in the deep-engraved lines of public gratitude, and in the respect and homage of mankind.

No two men now live, fellow-citizens, perhaps it may be doubted whether any two men have ever lived in one age, who, more than those we now commemorate, have impressed on mankind their own sentiments in regard to politics and government, infused their own opinions more deeply into the opinions of others, or given a more lasting direction to the current of human thought. Their work doth not perish with them. . . . No age will come in which the American Revolution will appear less than it is, one of the greatest events in human history. No age will come in which it shall cease to be seen and felt, on either continent, that a great advance, not only in American affairs, but in human affairs, was made on the 4th of July, 1776.

As a composition, the Declaration [of Independence] is Mr. Jefferson's. It is the production of his mind, and the high honor of it belongs to him, clearly and absolutely.

The Congress of the Revolution, fellow-citizens, sat with closed doors, and no report of its debates was ever made. The discussion, therefore, which accompanied this great measure, has never been preserved, except in memory and by tradition. But it is, I believe, doing no injustice to others to say, that the general opinion was, and uniformly has been, that in debate, on the side of independence, John Adams had no equal. The great author of the Declaration himself had expressed that opinion uniformly and strongly.

Let us, then, bring before us the assembly,

which was about to decide a question thus big with the fate of empire. Let us open their doors and look in upon their deliberations. Let us survey the anxious and care-worn countenances, let us hear the firm-toned voices, of this band of .patriots.

Hancock presides over the solemn sitting ; and one of those not yet prepared to pronounce for absolute independence is on the floor, and is urging his reasons for dissenting from the Declaration. . . .

It was for Mr. Adams to reply to arguments like these. We know his opinions, and we know his character. He would commence with his accustomed directness and earnestness.

" Sink or swim, live or die, survive or perish, I give my hand and my heart to this vote. It is true, indeed, that in the beginning we aimed not at independence. But there's a Divinity which shapes our ends. The injustice of England has driven us to arms ; and, blinded to her own interest for our good, she has obstinately persisted, till independence is now within our grasp. . . . Read this Declaration at the head of the army; every sword will be drawn from its scabbard, and the solemn vow uttered, to maintain it, or to perish on the bed of honor. Publish it from the pulpit; religion will approve it, and the love of religious liberty will cling round it, resolved to stand with it, or fall with it. Send it to the public halls; proclaim it there; let them hear it who heard the first roar of the enemy's cannon; let them see it who saw their brothers and their sons fall on the field of Bunker Hill, and in the streets of Lexington and Concord, and the very walls will cry out in its support."

"Sir, I know the uncertainty of human affairs, but I see, I see clearly, through this day's business. You and I, indeed, may rue it. We may not live to the time when this Declaration shall be made good. We may die; die colonists; die slaves; die, it may be, ignominiously and on the scaffold. Be it so! Be it so! If it be the pleasure of Heaven that my country shall require the poor offering of my life, the victim shall be ready, at the appointed hour of sacrifice, come when that hour may. But while I do live, let me have a country, or at least the hope of a country, and that a free country. . . . We shall make this a glorious, an immortal day. When we are in our graves, our children will honor it. They will celebrate it with thanksgiving, with festivity, with bonfires, and illuminations. . . . Sir, before God, I believe the hour is come. My judgment approves this measure, and my whole heart is in it. All that I have, and all that I am, and all that I hope, in this life, I am now ready here to stake upon it ; and I leave off as I begun, that live or die, survive or perish, I am for the Declaration. It is my living sentiment, and by the blessing of God it shall be my dying sentiment,—Independence *now*, and INDEPENDENCE FOR EVER !''

And so that day shall be honored, illustrious prophet and patriot ! so that day shall be honored, and as often as it returns, thy renown shall come along with it, and the glory of thy life, like the day of thy death, shall not fail from the remembrance of men.

THE REPLY TO HAYNE, OF SOUTH CAROLINA. Jan. 26 and 27, 1830.

I shall not acknowledge that the honorable member goes before me in regard for whatever of distinguished talent or distinguished character South Carolina has produced. I claim part of the honor, I partake in the pride, of her great names. I claim them for countrymen, one and all, the Laurenses, the Rutledges, the Pinckneys, the Sumpters, the Marions, Americans all, whose fame is no more to be hemmed in by State lines, than their talents and patriotism were capable of being circumscribed within the same narrow limits. In their day and generation, they served and honored the country, and the whole country; and their renown is of the treasures of the whole country.

Mr. President, I shall enter on no encomium upon Massachusetts; she needs none. There she is. Behold her, and judge for yourselves. There is her history; the world knows it by heart. The past, at least, is secure. There is Boston, and Concord, and Lexington, and Bunker Hill; and there they will remain forever. The bones of her sons, falling in the great struggle for Independence, now lie mingled with the soil of every State from New England to Georgia; and there they will lie forever. And, Sir, where American liberty raised its first voice, and where its youth was nurtured and sustained, there it still lives, in the strength of its manhood and full of its original spirit. If discord and disunion shall wound it, if party strife and blind ambition shall hawk at and tear it, if folly and madness, if uneasiness under salutary and necessary restraint, shall succeed in separating it from the Union, by which alone its existence is made sure, it will stand, in the end, by the side of that cradle in which its infancy was rocked; it will stretch forth its arm with whatever of vigor it may still retain over the friends who gather around it; and it will fall at last, if fall it must, amidst the proudest monuments of its own glory, and on the very spot of its origin.

The inherent right in the people to reform their government I do not deny : and they have another right, and that is, to resist unconstitutional laws, without overturning the government. It is no doctrine of mine that unconstitutional laws bind the people.

The right of a State to annul a law of Congress cannot be maintained, but on the ground of the inalienable right of man to resist oppression ; that is to say, upon the ground of revolution. I admit that there is an ultimate violent remedy, above the Constitution and in defiance of the Constitution, which may be resorted to when a revolution is to be justified. But I do not admit, that, under the Constitution and in conformity with it, there is any mode in which a State government, as a member of the Union, can interfere and stop the progress of the general government, by force of her own laws, under any circumstances whatever.

The people have wisely provided, in the Constitution itself, a proper, suitable mode and tribunal for settling questions of Constitutional law. . . . The Constitution itself has pointed out, ordained, and established that authority. How has it accomplished this great and essential end? By declaring, Sir, that "*the Constitution, and the laws of the United States made in pursuance thereof, shall be the supreme law of the land, anything in the Constitution or laws of any State to the contrary notwithstanding.*" . . . . But who shall decide this question of interference? To whom lies the last appeal? This, Sir, the Constitution itself decides also, by declaring, that "*the judicial power shall extend to all cases arising under the Constitution and laws of the United States.*" These two provisions cover the whole ground. They are, in truth, the keystone of the arch! With these it is a government; without them it is a confederation.

When my eyes shall be turned to behold for the last time the sun in heaven, may I not see him shining on the broken and dishonored fragments of a once glorious Union; on States dissevered, discordant, belligerent; on a land rent with civil feuds, or drenched. it may be, in fraternal blood! Let their last feeble and lingering glance rather behold the gorgeous ensign of the republic, now known and honored throughout the earth, still full high advanced, its arms and trophies streaming in their original luster, not a stripe erased or polluted, nor a single star obscured, bearing for its motto, no such miserable interrogatory as "What is all this worth?" nor those other words of delusion and folly, "Liberty first and Union afterwards;" but everywhere, spread all over in characters of living light, blazing on all its ample folds, as they float over the sea and over the land, and in every wind under the whole heavens, that other sentiment, dear to every true American heart,—Liberty *and* Union, now and for ever, one and inseparable!

THE CONSTITUTION NOT A COMPACT.
February 16, 1833.

SIR, I love Liberty no less ardently than the gentleman himself, in whatever form she may have appeared in the progress of human history. As exhibited in the master states of antiquity, as breaking out again from amidst the darkness of the Middle Ages, and beaming on the formation of new communities in modern Europe, she has, always and everywhere, charms for me. Yet, Sir, it is our own liberty, guarded by constitutions and secured by Union, it is that liberty which is our paternal inheritance, it is our established, dear-sought, peculiar American liberty, to which I am chiefly devoted, and the cause of which I now mean, to the utmost of my power, to maintain and defend.

The first resolution declares that the people of the United States "*acceded*" to the Constitution, or to the constitutional compact, as it is called. This word "accede," not found either in the Constitution itself, or in the ratification of it by any one of the States, has been chosen for use here, doubtless, not without a well-considered purpose.

The natural converse of *accession* is *scces-*

sion; and, therefore when it is stated that
the people of the States acceded to the
Union, it may be more plausibly argued,
that they may secede from it. . . . The
people of the United States have used no
such form of expression in establishing the
present government. They do not say that
they *accede* to a league, but they declare
that they *ordain* and *establish* a Consti-
tion. . . . Inasmuch as they were already
in union, they did not speak of *acceding* to
the new Articles of Confederation, but of
ratifying and confirming them; . . . .
No State is at liberty to *secede*, on the
ground that she and other States have done
nothing but *accede*. She must show that she
has a right to *reverse* what has been
ordained, to *unsettle* and *overthrow* what
has been *established*, to *reject* what the
people have *adopted*, and to *break up* what
they have *ratified*; because these are the
terms which express the transactions which
have actually taken place. In other words,
she must show her right to make a revolution.

To begin with nullification, with the avowed intent, nevertheless, not to proceed to secession, dismemberment, and general revolution, is as if one were to take the plunge of Niagara, and cry out that he would stop half-way down. In the one case, as in the other, the rash adventurer must go to the bottom of the dark abyss below, were it not that that abyss has no discovered bottom.

PUBLIC DINNER IN NEW YORK.
March 10, 1831.

Who is there among us, that, should he find himself on any spot of the earth where human beings exist, and where the existence of other nations is known, would not be proud to say, I am an American? I am a countryman of Washington? I am a citizen of that republic, which, although it has suddenly sprung up, yet there are none on the globe who have ears to hear, and have not heard of it; who have eyes to see, and have not read of it; who know anything, and yet do not know of its existence and its glory?

There are two principles, Gentlemen, strictly and purely American, which are now likely to prevail throughout the civilized world. Indeed, they seem the necessary result of the progress of civilization and knowledge. These are, first, popular governments, restrained by written constitutions; and secondly, universal education. Popular governments and general education, acting and reacting, mutually producing and reproducing each other, are the mighty agencies which in our days appear to be exciting, stimulating, and changing civilized societies. Man, everywhere, is now found demanding a participation in government,—and he will not be refused : and demands knowledge as necessary to self-government.

THE CHARACTER OF WASHINGTON (Centennial Anniversary). Feb. 22, 1832.

One of the most striking things ever said of him is, that " *he changed mankind's ideas of political greatness.*"[1] To commanding talents, and to success, the common

---

[1] Fisher Ames.

elements of such greatness, he added a disregard of self, a spotlessness of motive, a ready submission to every public and private duty, which threw far into the shade the whole crowd of vulgar great, ... His love of glory, so far as that may be supposed to have influenced him at all, spurned everything short of general approbation. It would have been nothing to him, that his partisans or his favorites outnumbered, or outvoted, or outmanaged, or outclamored, those of other leaders. He had no favorites ; he rejected all partisanship : and, acting honestly for the universal good, he deserved, what he has so richly enjoyed, the universal love.

His fame is as durable as his principles, as lasting as truth and virtue themselves. While the hundreds whom party excitement, and temporary circumstances, and casual combinations, have raised into transient notoriety, sink again, like thin bubbles, bursting and dissolving into the great ocean, Washington's fame is like the rock which bounds that ocean, and at whose feet its billows are destined to break harmlessly for ever.

Washington, therefore, could regard, and did regard, nothing as of paramount political interest, but the integrity of the Union itself. With a united government, well administered, he saw that we had nothing to fear ; and without it, nothing to hope. The sentiment is just, and its momentous truth should solemnly impress the whole country.

Executive Patronage and Removals from Office. October 12, 1836.

Mr. President, as far as I know, there is no civilized country on earth, in which, on a change of rulers, there is such an *inquisition for spoil* as we have witnessed in this free republic.

This principle of claiming a monopoly of office by the right of conquest, unless the public shall effectually rebuke and restrain it, will entirely change the character of our government. It elevates party above country; it forgets the common weal in the pursuit of personal emolument; it tends to form, it does form, we see that it has formed, a political combination, united by no common principles or opinions among its members, either upon the powers of the government, or the true policy of the country; but held together simply as an association, under the charm of a popular head, seeking to maintain possession of the government by a *vigorous exercise of its patronage*; . . . . Sir, if this course of things cannot be checked, good men will grow tired of the exercise of political privileges. They will have nothing to do with popular elections. They will see that such elections are but a mere selfish contest for office; and they will abandon the government to the scramble of the bold, the daring, and the desperate.

In all popular governments, a FREE PRESS is the most important of all agents and instruments. . . . While it acts in a manner worthy of this distinction, the press is a fountain of light, and a source of gladdening warmth. It instructs the public mind, and animates the spirit of patriotism. . . . But remember, Sir, that these are the attributes of a FREE press only. And is a press that is purchased or pensioned more free than a press that is fettered? Can the people look for truths to partial sources, whether rendered partial through fear or through favor?

An open attempt to secure the aid and friendship of the public press, by bestowing the emoluments of office on its active conductors, seems to me, of everything we have witnessed, to be the most reprehensible. It degrades both the government and the press.

SPEECH ON BANKING.

January 31, 1834.

The very man, of all others, who has the deepest interest in a sound currency, and who suffers most by mischievous legislation in money matters, is the man who earns his daily bread by his daily toil. A depreciated currency, sudden changes of prices, paper money, falling between morning and noon, and falling still lower between noon and night,—these things constitute the very harvest-time of speculators, and of the whole race of those who are at once idle and crafty ; and of that other race, too, the Catilines of all times, marked, so as to be known for ever, by one stroke of the historian's pen, *those greedy of other men's property and prodigal of their own.*

Whoever attempts, under whatever popular cry, to shake the stability of the public currency, bring on distress in money matters, and drive the country into the use of paper money, stabs your interest and your happiness to the heart.

RECEPTION AT NEW YORK.
March 15, 1837.

He who tampers with the currency robs labor of its bread. He panders, indeed, to greedy capital, which is keen-sighted, and may shift for itself ; but he beggars labor, which is honest, unsuspecting, and too busy for the present to calculate for the future.

Did wild schemes and projects ever benefit the industrious? Did irredeemable bank paper ever enrich the laborious? Did violent fluctuations ever do good to him who depends on his daily labor for his daily bread? Certainly never. All these things may gratify greediness for sudden gain, or the rashness of daring speculation; but they can bring nothing but injury and distress to the homes of patient industry and honest labor.

REPLY TO MR. CALHOUN.
March 22, 1838.

The Secretary of the Treasury . . . . assures us, that, bad as the times were, and notwithstanding the floods of bad paper which deluged the country, members of Congress should get gold and silver. . . . If there be bad money in the country, I think that Secretaries and other executive officers, and especially the members of Congress, should be the last to receive any good money ; because they have the power, if they will do their duty, and exercise it, of making the money of the country good for all.

"THE LOG CABIN CANDIDATE." [Wm. Henry Harrison.] August 12, 1840.

It touched a tender point in the public feeling. It naturally roused indignation. What was intended as reproach was immediately seized on as merit. " Be it so ! Be it so !" was the instant burst of the public voice. "Let him be the log-cabin candidate." . . . . It is only shallow-minded pretenders who either make distinguished origin matter of personal merit, or obscure origin matter of personal reproach. . . . A man who is not ashamed of himself need not be ashamed of his early condition.

ADDRESS TO THE LADIES OF RICHMOND. October 5, 1840.

We applaud the artist whose skill and genius present the mimic man upon the canvas ; we admire and celebrate the sculptor who works out that same image in enduring marble; but how insignificant are these achievements, though the highest and the fairest in all the departments of art, in comparison with the great vocation of human mothers ! They work not upon the canvas that shall perish, or the marble that crumbles into dust, but upon mind, upon spirit, which is to last for ever, and which is to bear, for good or evil, throughout its duration, the impress of a mother's plastic hand.

RECEPTION AT BOSTON.
September 30, 1842.

Every settlement of national differences between Christian states by fair negotiation, without resort to arms, is a new illustration and a new proof of the benign influence of the Christian faith.

Repudiation does nothing but add a sort of disrepute to acknowledged inability.

THE LANDING AT PLYMOUTH.
December 22, 1843.

Circumstances have wrought out for us a

state of things which, in other times and other regions, philosophy has dreamed of, and theory has proposed, and speculation has suggested, but which man has never been able to accomplish. I mean the government of a great nation over a vastly extended portion of the surface of the earth, *by means of local institutions for local purposes*, and *general institutions for general purposes.*

I care not beneath what zone, frozen, temperate, or torrid ; I care not of what complexion, white or brown ; I care not under what circumstances of climate or cultivation,—if I can find a race of men on an inhabitable spot of earth whose general sentiment it is, and whose general feeling it is, that government is made for man,—man, as a religious, moral, and social being,—and not man for government, there I know that I shall find prosperity and happiness.

THE GIRARD WILL CASE.
Philadelphia, February 20, 1844.

No literary efforts, no adjudications, no

constitutional discussions, nothing that has been said or done in favor of the great interests of universal man, has done this country more credit, at home and abroad, than the establishment of our body of clergymen, their support by voluntary contributions, and the general excellence of their character for piety and learning.

The great truth has thus been proclaimed and proved, a truth which I believe will in time to come shake all the hierarchies of Europe, that the voluntary support of such a ministry, under free institutions, is a practicable idea.

THE RHODE ISLAND GOVERNMENT.
January 27, 1848.

What distinguishes American governments as much as any thing else from any governments of ancient or of modern times, is the marvelous felicity of their representative system. . . . The power is with the people ; but they cannot exercise it in masses or *per capita* ; they can only exercise it by their representatives. The whole system with us has been popular from the beginning.

We are not to take the will of the people from public meetings, nor from tumultuous assemblies, by which the timid are terrified, the prudent are alarmed, and by which society is disturbed. These are not American modes of signifying the will of the people, and they never were. . . . What is this but anarchy? What liberty is there here, but a tumultuary, tempestuous, violent, stormy liberty, a sort of South American liberty, without power except in its spasms, a liberty supported by arms to-day, crushed by arms to-morrow? Is that *our* liberty?

All that is necessary here is, that the will of the people should be ascertained, by some regular rule of proceeding, prescribed by previous law. . . . and thence arises the necessity for suffrage, which is the mode whereby each man's power is made to tell upon the constitution of the government, and in the enactment of laws.

SPEECH AT MARSHFIELD.

September 1, 1848.

At this moment, there is no object upon earth so much attracting the gaze of the intelligent and civilized nations of the earth as this great republic. All men look at us, all men examine our course. . . . They see us as that star of empire which half a century ago was represented as making its way westward. I wish they may see it as a mild, placid, though brilliant orb, moving athwart the whole heavens to the enlightening and cheering of mankind ; and not as a meteor of fire and blood terrifying the nations.

FOR THE CONSTITUTION AND THE UNION. March 7, 1850.

Secession ! Peaceable session ! Sir, your eyes and mine are never destined to see that miracle. The dismemberment of this vast country without convulsion ! The breaking up of the fountains of the great deep without ruffling the surface ! Who is so foolish, I beg everybody's pardon, as to expect to see any such thing ? Sir, he who sees these States, now revolving in harmony around a common center, and expects to see them quit their places and fly off without convulsion, may look the next hour to see the heavenly bodies rush from their spheres, and jostle against each other in the realms of space, without causing the wreck of the universe.

No, sir ! No, sir ! I will not state what might produce the disruption of the Union ; but, Sir, I see as plainly as I see the sun in heaven what that disruption itself must produce ; I see that it must produce war, and such a war as I will not describe.

RECEPTION AT BUFFALO.
May 22, 1851.

I believe in party distinctions. I am a party man. There are questions belonging to party in which I take an interest, and there are opinions entertained by other parties which I repudiate ; but what of all that ? If a house be divided against itself, it will fall, and crush everybody in it. We must

see that we maintain the government which
is over us.   We must see that we uphold the
Constitution, and we must do so without regard to party.

THE ADDITION TO THE CAPITOL.
July 4, 1851.

I will venture. . . . to state, in a few
words, what I take these American political
principles in substance to be.   They consist,
as I think, in the first place, in the establishment of popular governments, on the basis
of representation ; . . . The next fundamental principle in our system is, that the
will of the majority, fairly expressed through
the means of representation, shall have the
force of law. . . . And, as the necessary
result of this, the third element is, that the
law is the supreme rule for the government
of all. . . . And, finally, another most
important part of the great fabric of American liberty is, that there shall be written
constitutions, founded on the immediate authority of the people themselves, and regu-
lating and restraining all the powers conferred

upon government, whether legislative, executive, or judicial.

This, fellow-citizens, I suppose to be a just summary of our American principles.

And I now proceed to add, that the strong and deep-settled conviction of all intelligent persons amongst us is, that, in order to support a useful and wise government upon these popular principles, the general education of the people, and the wide diffusion of pure morality and true religion, are indispensable. Individual virtue is a part of public virtue.

I now do declare, in the face of all the intelligent of the age, that, for the period which has elapsed from the day that Washington laid the foundation of this Capitol to the present time, there has been no country upon earth in which life, liberty, and property have been more amply and steadily secured, or more freely enjoyed, than in these United States of America. . . . Who is there that can stand upon the foundation of facts, acknowledged or proved, and assert that these our republican institutions have not answered the true ends of government beyond all precedent in human history?

We cannot, we dare not, we will not betray our sacred trust. . . . The bow that gilds the clouds in the heavens, the pillars that uphold the firmament, may disappear and fall away in the hour appointed by the will of God ; but until that day comes, or so long as our lives may last, no ruthless hand shall undermine that bright arch of Union and Liberty which spans the continent from Washington to California.

And now, fellow-citizens, with hearts void of hatred, envy, and malice towards our own countrymen, or any of them, or towards the subjects or citizens of other governments, or towards any member of the great family of man ; but exulting, nevertheless, in our own peace, security, and happiness, in the grateful remembrance of the past, and the glorious hopes of the future, let us return to our homes, and with humility and devotion offer our thanks to the Father of all our mercies, political, social, and religious.

ABRAHAM LINCOLN.

Here was a type of the true elder race,
And one of Plutarch's men talked with us, face to face.
                              —JAMES RUSSELL LOWELL.

NEW SALEM, ILLS.

June 13, 1836.

To the Editor of the Journal:—

In your paper of last Saturday, I see a communication over the signature of " Many Voters," in which the candidates who are announced in the *Journal* are called upon to " show their hands." Agreed. Here's mine.

I go for all sharing the privileges of the government who assist in bearing its burdens ; consequently, I go for admitting all whites to the right of suffrage who pay taxes or bear arms (by no means excluding females).

If elected I shall consider the whole people of Sangamon my constituents, as well those that oppose as those that support me.

SPEECH AT SPRINGFIELD, ILLS.

June 26, 1857.

I think the authors of that notable instrument [the Declaration of Independence] intended to include *all* men, but they did not intend to declare all men equal *in all respects.* They did not mean to say all were equal in color, size, intellect, moral developments, or social capacity. They defined with tolerable distinctness in what respects they did consider all men created equal— equal with " certain inalienable rights, among which are life, liberty, and the pursuit of happiness." This they said, and this they meant. They did not mean to assert the obvious untruth that all men were then actually enjoying that equality, nor yet that they were about to confer it immediately upon them. In fact, they had no power to confer such a boon. They meant simply to declare the right, so that the enforcement of it might follow as fast as circumstances should permit.

SPEECH AT SPRINGFIELD, ILLS.

June 16, 1858.

In my opinion, it [agitation] will not cease until a crisis shall have been reached and passed. " A house divided against itself can not stand." [1] I believe this government can not endure permanently half slave and half free. I do not expect the Union to be dissolved—I do not expect the house to fall—but I do expect it will cease to be divided. It will become all one thing, or all the other. Either the opponents of slavery will arrest the further spread of it, and place it where the public mind shall rest in the belief that it is in course of ultimate extinction ; or its advocates will push it forward till it shall become alike lawful in all the States, old as well as new, North as well as South.

SPEECH AT CHICAGO.

July 10, 1858.

Those arguments that are made, that the

---

[1] See Webster, p. 119.

inferior race are to be treated with as much
allowance as they are capable of enjoying;
that as much is to be done for them as their
condition will allow—what are these arguments? They are the arguments that kings
have made for enslaving the people in all
ages of the world. You will find that all
the arguments in favor of king-craft were of
this class; they always bestrode the necks
of the people—not that they wanted to do it,
but because the people were better off for
being ridden.

DOUGLAS DEBATE.
October 7, 1858.

If you will take the Judge's [Douglas's]
speeches, and select the short and pointed sen-
tences expressed by him,—as his declaration
that he "don't care whether slavery is voted
up or down" [in the Territories],—you will
see at once that this is perfectly logical, if
you do not admit that slavery is wrong.
If you do admit that it is wrong,
Judge Douglas cannot logically say he don't
care whether a wrong is voted up or voted

down. . . . he cannot logically say that anybody has a right to do wrong.

To Republicans of Boston, Mass.
April 6, 1859.

This is a world of compensations; and he who would be no slave must consent to have no slave. Those who deny freedom to others deserve it not for themselves ; and under a just God, can not long retain it.

Cooper Institute Speech, New York.
February 27, 1860.

I do not mean to say we are bound to follow implicitly in whatever our fathers did. To do so, would be to discard all the lights of current experience—to reject all progress, all improvement. What I do say is that if we would supplant the opinions and policy of our fathers in any case, we should do so upon evidence so conclusive, and argument so clear, that even their great authority, fairly considered and weighed, can not stand.

Some of you [Southerners] delight to flaunt in our faces the warning against sectional parties given by Washington in his Farewell Address. Less than eight years before Washington gave that warning, he had, as President of the United States, approved and signed an act of Congress enforcing the prohibition of slavery in the North-Western Territory, which act embodied the policy of the government upon that subject, up to and at the very moment he penned that warning ; and about one year after he penned it he wrote La Fayette that he considered that prohibition a wise measure, expressing in the same connection his hope that we should some time have a confederacy of free States.

Bearing this in mind, and seeing that sectionalism has still arisen upon this same subject, is that warning a weapon in your hands against us, or in our hands against you? Could Washington himself speak, would he cast the blame of that sectionalism upon us, who sustain his policy, or upon you, who repudiate it? We respect that warning of Washington, and we commend it to you together with his example pointing to the right application of it.

Wrong as we think slavery is, we can yet afford to let it alone where it is, because that much is due to the necessity arising from its actual presence in the nation; but can we, while our votes will prevent it, allow it to spread into the national Territories, and to overrun us here in these free States? If our sense of duty forbids this, then let us stand by our duty, fearlessly and effectively. Let us be diverted by none of those sophistical contrivances wherewith we are so industriously plied and belabored—contrivances such as groping for some middle ground between right and wrong: vain as the search for a man who should be neither a living man nor a dead man; such as a policy of " don't care " on a question about which all true men do care.

ON HIS WAY TO WASHINGTON AS PRESIDENT ELECT. February, 1861.

At Columbus, O.—It is true, as has been

said by the President of the Senate, that very great responsibility rests upon me in the position to which the votes of the American people have called me. I am deeply sensible of that weighty responsibility. I cannot but know what you all know, that without a name, perhaps without a reason why I should have a name, there has fallen upon me a task such as did not rest even upon the Father of his Country, and so feeling, I can turn and look for that support without which it will be impossible for me to perform that great task. I turn, then, and look to the great American people, and to that God who has never forsaken them.

At Philadelphia.—Your worthy mayor has expressed the wish, in which I join with him, that it were convenient for me to remain in your city long enough for me to consult your merchants and manufacturers ; or, as it were, to listen to those breathings rising within the consecrated walls wherein the Constitution of the United States, and, I will add, the Declaration of Independence, were originally framed and adopted. I assure you and your mayor that I had hoped on this occasion, and upon all occasions during my life, that I shall do nothing inconsistent with the teachings of these holy and most sacred walls. I have never asked anything that does not breathe from those walls. All my political warfare has been in favor of the teachings that come forth from these sacred walls. May my right hand forget its cunning and my tongue cleave to the roof of my mouth if ever I prove false to those teachings !

I have often inquired of myself what great principle or idea it was that kept this Confederacy so long together. It was not the mere matter of the separation of the colonies from the motherland, but that sentiment in the Declaration of Independence which gave liberty, not alone to the people of this country, but hope to all the world, for all future time. . . . Now, my friends, can this country be saved on that basis ? If it can, I will consider myself one of the happiest men in the world if I can help to save it. If it cannot be saved upon that principle, it will be truly awful. But if this country cannot be saved without giving up that principle, I was about to say I would rather be assassinated on this spot than surrender it.

My friends, this is wholly an unprepared speech. I did not expect to be called on to say a word when I came here. I supposed I was merely to do something toward raising a flag; I may, therefore, have said something indiscreet. But I have said nothing but what I am willing to live by, and, if it be the pleasure of Almighty God, to die by.

FIRST INAUGURAL ADDRESS.

March 4, 1861.

A disruption of the Federal Union, heretofore only menaced, is now formidably attempted. I hold that in the contemplation of universal law and of the Constitution, the

Union of these States is perpetual. Perpetuity is implied, if not expressed, in the fundamental law of all national governments. It is safe to assert that no government proper ever had a provision in its organic law for its termination.

If the United States be not a government proper, but an association of States in the nature of a contract merely, can it, as a contract, be peaceably unmade by less than all the parties who made it? One party to a contract may violate it—break it, so to speak; but does it not require all to lawfully rescind it? Descending from these general principles, we find the proposition that, in legal contemplation the Union is perpetual confirmed by the history of the Union itself.

It follows from these views that no State, upon its own mere motion can lawfully get out of the Union; that resolves and ordinances to that effect are legally void; and that acts of violence, within any State or States, against the authority of the United States, are insurrectionary or revolutionary, according to circumstances.

I therefore consider that, in view of the Constitution and the laws, the Union is unbroken ; and to the extent of my ability I shall take care, as the Constitution itself expressly enjoins upon me, that the laws ot the Union shall be faithfully executed in all the States.

In doing this there needs to be no bloodshed or violence ; and there shall be none, unless it be forced upon the national authority.

The power confided to me will be used to hold, occupy, and possess the property and places belonging to the government, and to collect the duties and imposts ; but beyond what may be necessary for these objects, there will be no invasion, no using of force against or among the people anywhere.

No organic law can ever be framed with a provision specifically applicable to every question which may occur in practical ad-- ministration. No foresight can anticipate, nor any document of reasonable length contain, express provisions for all possible questions. Shall fugitives from labor be surrendered by national or by State authority? The Constitution does not expressly say. *May* Congress prohibit slavery in the Territories? The Constitution does not expressly say. *Must* Congress protect slavery in the Territories? The Constitution does not expressly say. From questions of this class spring all our constitutional controversies, and we divide upon them into majorities and minorities.

If the minority will not acquiesce, the majority must, or the government must cease. There is no other alternative; for continuing the government is acquiescence on one side or the other. If a minority in such case will secede rather than acquiesce, they make a precedent which, in turn, will divide and ruin them; for a minority of their own will secede from them whenever a majority refuses to be controlled by such a minority.

A majority held in constraint by constitutional checks and limitations, and always changing easily with deliberate changes of popular opinions and sentiments, is the only true sovereign of a free people. Whoever rejects it does, of necessity, fly to anarchy or to despotism.

Physically speaking, we can not separate; we cannot remove our respective sections from each other, nor build an impassable wall between them. A husband and wife may be divorced, and go out of the presence and beyond the reach of each other ; but the different parts of our country can not do this. They can not but remain face to face, and intercourse, either amicable or hostile, must continue between them. Is it possible, then, to make that intercourse more advantageous or more satisfactory after separation than before ?

The Chief Magistrate derives all his authority from the people, and they have conferred none upon him to fix the term for the separation of the States. The people themselves can do this also if they choose ; but the executive, as such, has nothing to do with it. His duty is to administer the present government, as it came to his hands, and to transmit it, unimpaired by him, to his successor.

By the frame of the government under which we live, this same people have wisely given their public servants but little power for mischief ; and have, with equal wisdom, provided for the return of that little to their own hands at very short intervals. While the people retain their virtue and vigilance, no administration, by any extreme of wickedness or folly, can very seriously injure the government in the short space of four years.

My countrymen, one and all, think calmly and well upon this whole subject. Nothing valuable can be lost by taking time. If there be an object to hurry any of you, in hot haste, to a step which you would never take deliberately, that object will be frustrated by taking time; but no good object can be frustrated by it.

In your hands, my dissatisfied fellow-countrymen, and not in mine, is the momentous issue of civil war. The government will not assail you. You can have no conflict without being yourselves the aggressors. You have no oath registered in Heaven to destroy the government; while I shall have the most solemn one to "preserve, protect, and defend it."

I am loath to close. We are not enemies, but friends. We must not be enemies. Though passion may have strained, it must not break our bonds of affection. The mystic chords of memory, stretching from every battlefield and patriot grave to every living heart and hearthstone all over this broad land, will yet swell the chorus of the Union when again touched, as surely they will be, by the better angels of our nature.

MESSAGE TO CONGRESS—SPECIAL SESSION. July 4, 1861.

In this act, [the attack on Fort Sumter] discarding all else, they have forced upon the country the distinct issue : " immediate dissolution, or blood."

And this issue embraces more than the fate of these United States. It presents to the whole family of man the question, whether a constitutional republic, or democracy,—a government of the people, by the same people—can or cannot maintain its territorial integrity against its own domestic foes. . . . It forces us to ask : " Is there, in all republics, this inherent and fatal weakness ? " " Must a government of necessity be too strong for the liberties of its own people, or too weak to maintain its own existence ? "

It might seem, at first thought, to be of little difference whether the present movement at the South be called " secession " or " rebellion." The movers, however, well understand the difference. . . . They knew their people possessed as much of moral sense, as much of devotion to law and order and as much pride in and reverence for the history and government of their common country, as any other civilized and patriotic people. . . . They invented an ingenious sophism, which, if conceded, was followed by perfectly logical steps, through all the incidents, to the complete destruction of the Union. The sophism itself is, that any State of the Union may, consistently with the National Constitution, and therefore lawfully and peacefully, withdraw from the Union without the consent of the Union or of any other State.

What is a "sovereignty," in the political sense of the term? Would it be far wrong to define it "a political community, without a political superior"? Tested by this, no one of our States except Texas ever was a sovereignty. And even Texas gave up the character on coming into the Union.

The States have their status in the Union,

and they have no other legal status. If they break from this, they can only do so against law and by revolution. The Union, and not themselves separately, procured their independence and their liberty.

The nation purchased with money the countries out of which several of these States were formed. Is it just that they shall go off without leave, and without refunding? . . . . If one State may secede, so may another: and when all shall have seceded none is left to pay the debts. Is this quite just to creditors? Did we notify them of this sage view of ours when we borrowed their money?

Our popular Government has often been called an experiment. Two points in it our people have already settled—the successful establishing and the successful administering of it. One still remains—its successful maintenance against a formidable internal attempt to overthrow it.

It was with the greatest regret that the

executive found the duty of employing the war-power in defense of the government forced upon him. He could but perform this duty or surrender the existence of the government. No compromise by public servants could, in this case, be a cure ; not that compromises are not often proper, but that no popular government can long survive a marked precedent that those who carry an election can only save the Government from immediate destruction by giving up the main point upon which the people gave the election. The people themselves, and not their servants, can safely reverse their own deliberate decisions.

To Horace Greeley.

Aug. 22, 1862.

As to the policy I "seem to be pursuing," as you say, I have not meant to leave any one in doubt. I would save the Union. I would save it in the shortest way under the Constitution. . . . My paramount object is to save the Union, and not either to save or destroy slavery.

If I could save the Union without freeing any slave, I would do it : if I could save it by freeing all the slaves, I would do it; and if I could do it by freeing some and leaving others alone, I would also do that.

What I do about slavery and the colored race, I do because I believe it helps to save this Union ; and what I forbear, I forbear because I do not believe it would help to save the Union.

I shall do less whenever I shall believe what I am doing hurts the cause, and I shall do more whenever I believe doing more helps the cause. I shall try to correct errors when shown to be errors, and I shall adopt new views so fast as they shall appear to be true views.

PRELIMINARY PROCLAMATION OF EMAN-
CIPATION. September 22, 1862.

I, Abraham Lincoln, President of the United States of America, and commander-in-chief of the army and navy thereof, do hereby proclaim and declare that hereafter, as heretofore, the war will be prosecuted for the object of practically restoring the Constitutional relation between the United States and each of the States, and the people thereof, in which States that relation is or may be suspended or disturbed.

That it is my purpose, upon the next meeting of Congress, to again recommend the adoption of a practical measure tendering pecuniary aid to the free acceptance or rejection of all Slave States, so-called, the people whereof may not then be in rebellion against the United States, and which States may then have voluntarily adopted, or thereafter may voluntarily adopt, immediate or gradual abolishment of slavery within their respective limits ; . . . .

That on the first day of January, in the year of our Lord one thousand eight hundred and sixty-three, all persons held as slaves within any State or designated part of a State the people whereof shall then be in rebellion against the United States, shall be then, thenceforward, and forever free ; and the Executive Government of the United

States, including the military and naval authority thereof, will recognize and maintain the freedom of such persons, and will do no act or acts to repress such persons, or any of them, in any efforts they may make for their actual freedom.

SECOND ANNUAL MESSAGE TO CONGRESS.
December 1, 1862.

A nation may be said to consist of its territory, its people, and its laws. The territory is the only part which is of certain durability. " One generation passeth away, and another generation cometh, but the earth abideth forever." It is of the first importance to duly consider and estimate this ever-enduring part. . . .

Our national strife springs not from our permanent part, not from the land we inhabit, not from our national homestead. There is no possible severing of this but would multiply, and not mitigate, evils among us. In all its adaptations and aptitudes it demands union and abhors separation. In fact, it would ere long force re-

union, however much of blood and treasure
the separation might have cost.

Our strife pertains to ourselves—to the
passing generations of men ; and it can, without convulsion, be hushed forever with the
passing of one generation.

[This Message proposed a Constitutional
Amendment offering compensation by the
United States to all States which should
abolish slavery before January 1, 1900 ; confirming the liberty of all slaves freed by the
chances of war, with compensation to loyal
owners ; and providing for governmental
aid in colonizing free colored persons with
their own consent. This proposition arose
from Mr. Lincoln's sense of justice to the
loyal slave-holding Border States, and was
meant to provide against the inevitable destruction of their slave-property when the
Final Proclamation should be made. But
Congress did not second him, and nothing
came of it.]

Fellow-citizens, we can not escape history. We, of this Congress and this Ad-

ministration, will be remembered in spite of ourselves. No personal significance or insignificance can spare one or another of us. The fiery trial through which we pass will light us down, in honor or dishonor, to the latest generation. We say we are for the Union. The world will not forget that we say this. We know how to save the Union. The world knows we do know how to save it. We—even we here—hold the power and bear the responsibility. In giving freedom to the slave we assure freedom to the free—honorable alike in what we give and what we preserve. We shall nobly save or meanly lose the last, best hope of earth. Other means may succeed; this could not fail. The way is plain, peaceful, generous, just,—a way which, if followed, the world will forever applaud, and God must forever bless.

FINAL EMANCIPATION PROCLAMATION.
January 1st, 1863.

·I, Abraham Lincoln, President of the United States, by virtue of the power in me

vested as commander-in-chief of the army
and navy of the United States, in time of
actual armed rebellion against the authority
and government of the United States, and
as a fit and necessary war measure for suppressing such rebellion, do, on this first day
of January, in the year of our Lord one
thousand eight hundred and sixty-three, and
in accordance with my purpose so to do,
publicly proclaimed for the full period of
100 days, from the day first above men-
tioned, order and designate as the States
and parts of States wherein the people
thereof, respectively, are this day in rebellion
against the United States, the following,
to wit : . . . .

And by virtue of the power and for the purpose aforesaid, I do order and declare that
all persons held as slaves within said
designated States and parts of States, are,
and henceforward shall be, free ; and that
the Executive Government of the United
States, including the military and naval
authorities, thereof, will recognize and
maintain the freedom of said persons. . . .

And upon this act, sincerely believed to be an act of justice, warranted by the Constitution upon military necessity, I invoke the considerate judgment of mankind, and the gracious favor of Almighty God.

To The Working-Men of Manchester England. January 19, 1863.

I have the honor to acknowledge the address and resolutions which you sent me on the eve of the New Year. . . . I know and deeply deplore the sufferings which the working-men at Manchester and in all Europe, are called to endure in this crisis. . . . Through the action of our disloyal citizens, the working-men of Europe have been subjected to severe trials, for the purpose of forcing their sanction to that attempt. Under the circumstances I cannot but regard your decisive utterances as an instance of sublime Christian heroism which has not been surpassed in any age or in any country. . . . I do not doubt that the sentiments you have expressed will be sustained by your great nation ; and on the other hand, I have no hesitation in assuring you that they will excite admiration, esteem, and the most reciprocal feelings of friendship among the American people.

To General John M. Schofield.
[As to Missouri.] May 27, 1863

Let your military measures be strong enough to repel the invader and keep the peace, and not so strong as to unnecessarily harrass and persecute the people. It is a difficult rôle, and so much greater will be the honor if you perform it well. If both factions, or neither, shall abuse you, you will probably be about right. Beware of being assailed by one and praised by the other.

The Gettysburg Address.
November 19, 1863.

Forescore and seven years ago our fathers brought forth upon this continent, a new nation, conceived in liberty, and dedicated to the proposition that all men are created equal.

Now we are engaged in a great civil

war, testing whether that nation, or any nation so conceived and so dedicated, can long endure. We are met on a great battle-field of that war. We have come to dedicate a portion of that field, as a final resting-place for those who here gave their lives that that nation might live. It is altogether fitting and proper that we should do this.

But, in a larger sense, we can not dedi-cate—we can not consecrate—we can not hallow—this ground. The brave men, living and dead, who struggled here, have conse-crated it, far above our poor power to add or detract. The world will little note, nor long remember what we say here, but it can never forget what they did here. It is for us, the living, rather, to be dedicated here to the unfinished work which they who fought here have thus far so nobly advanced. It is rather for us to be here dedicated to the great task remaining before us—that from these honored dead we take increased devo-tion to that cause for which they gave the last full measure of devotion ; that we here highly resolve that these dead shall not have died in vain ; that this nation under God, shall have a new birth of freedom ; and that government of the people, by the people, for the people, shall not perish from the earth.

To A. G. Hodges.
April 4, 1864.

I claim not to have controlled events, but confess plainly that events have controlled me. . . . If God now wills the removal of a great wrong, and wills also that we of the North, as well as you of the South, shall pay fairly for our complicity in that wrong, impartial history will find therein new cause to attest and revere the justice and goodness of God.

Informal Speech, After His Second Election.   November 10, 1864.

The election, along with its incidental and undesirable strife, has done good, too. It has demonstrated that a people's government can sustain a national election in the midst of a great civil war. Until now, it has not been known to the world that this was a possibility. . . . It shows, also, to the extent yet known, that we have more men now than we had when the war began. Gold is good in its place, but living, brave, patriotic men, are better than gold.

FOURTH ANNUAL MESSAGE TO CONGRESS. December 6, 1864.

In stating a single condition of peace, I mean simply to say, that the war will cease on the part of the government whenever it shall have ceased on the part of those who began it.

SECOND INAUGURAL ADDRESS.

March 4, 1865.

Neither party expected for the war the magnitude or the duration which it has already attained. Neither anticipated that the cause of the conflict might cease with, or even before, the conflict itself should cease . . . . The Almighty has his own purposes . . . . Fondly do we hope—fervently do we pray—that this mighty scourge of war may speedily pass away. Yet, if God wills that it continue until all the wealth piled by the bondsman's two hundred and fifty years of unrequited toil shall be sunk, and until every drop of blood drawn with the lash shall be paid by another drawn with the sword, as was said three thousand years ago, so still it must be said, "The judgments of the Lord are true and righteous altogether."

With malice toward none; with charity for all; [1] with firmness in the right, as God gives us to see the right, let us strive on to finish the work we are in; to bind up the nation's wounds; to care for him who shall have borne the battle, and for his widow, and his orphan —to do all which may achieve and cherish a just and lasting peace among ourselves, and with all nations.

TO THURLOW WEED.

March 15, 1865.

Every one likes a compliment. Thank you for yours on my little notification speech

---

[1] See Webster, page 122,

and on the recent inaugural address. I expect the latter to wear as well as—perhaps better than—anything I have produced ; but I believe it is not immediately popular. Men are not flattered by being shown that there has been a difference of purpose between the Almighty and them. . . . It is a truth which I thought needed to be told, and, as whatever of humiliation there is in it falls most directly on myself, I thought others might afford for me to tell it.

MR. LINCOLN'S LAST SPEECH.
April 11, 1865.

By these recent successes [the evacuation of Petersburg and Richmond, and Lee's Surrender] the reinauguration of the national authority—reconstruction—which has had a large share of thought from the first, is pressed much more closely upon our attention. It is fraught with great difficulty. Unlike a case of war between independent nations, there is no authorized organ for us to treat with—no one man has authority to give up the rebellion for any other man.

We simply must begin with and mould from disorganized and discordant elements. Nor is it a small additional embarrassment that we, the loyal people, differ among ourselves as to the mode, manner, and measure of reconstruction.

We all agree that the seceded States, so-called, are out of their proper practical relation with the Union, and that the sole object of the government, civil and military, in regard to those States, is to again get them into that proper practical relation. I believe that it is not only possible, but in fact easier to do this without deciding or even considering whether these States have ever been out of the Union, than with it. Finding themselves safely at home, it would be utterly immaterial whether they had ever been abroad. Let us all join in doing the acts necessary to restoring the proper practical relations between these States and the Union, and each forever after innocently indulge his own opinion whether in doing the acts he brought the States from without into the

Union, or only gave them proper assistance, they never having been out of it.

So great peculiarities pertain to each State, and such important and sudden changes occur in the same State, and withal so new and unprecedented is the whole case that no exclusive and inflexible plan can safely be precribed as to details and collaterals. Such exclusive and inflexible plan would surely become a new entanglement. Important principles may, and must, be inflexible.

HENRY WARD BEECHER.

"To his undying fame the world and his memory stand in no need of witnesses."
—WILLIAM EWART GLADSTONE.

SHALL WE COMPROMISE?

February 21, 1850.

These oppugnant elements, Slavery and Liberty,—inherent in our political system, animating our constitution, checkering our public policy, breeding in statesmen opposite principles of government, and making our whole wisdom of public legislation on many of the greatest questions cross-eyed and contradictory,—these elements are seeking each other's life. One or the other must die.

Let no man suppose that the contentions which now agitate the land have sprung from the rash procedure of a few men—the hot heads either of the North or of the South. We are in the midst of a collision not of men, but of principles and political institutions.

We believe that the compromises of the Constitution looked to the destruction of slavery and not to its establishment.

There never was a plainer question for the North. It is her duty openly, firmly, and forever to refuse to slavery another inch of territory, and to see that it never gets any by fraud. . . . The path of Duty, though a steep one, and often toilsome, is always straight and plain. Those are the labyrinthine roads, which, winding through sloughs and thickets, or embosked and dark, seek to find a way around the rocks and steeps, and to come to the gate of Success without climbing the hill of Difficulty.

ARTICLE IN THE *Independent* [Fremont Campaign]. June 26, 1856.

Mr. Buchanan, in his letter of acceptance, holds out to the North the ever grateful and always deceitful promise of *peace*. . . . Every vote for him is a vote for war. No doubt Mr. Buchanan may desire to administer for peace. But when a man has gone out into the rapids, what he *wishes* has very little to do with the question of his going over the falls. . . . The [Democratic] Platform lies before the public as a man-of-war lies peacefully at anchor. Her sides are still. Her decks are quiet. Her magazine sleeps. She is peaceful indeed, and yet she is stuffed full of materials that only need a quickening, and every port-hole will fly open, every cannon blaze, and the whole ship belch thunder and lightning with broadsides of death.

Until liberty controls the institutions of liberty, until freemen rule in the land of freedom, we shall have nothing but disturbance.

THE NATION'S DUTY TO SLAVERY.
October 30, 1859.
After JOHN BROWN'S Raid.

I certainly think that even slaves would be made immeasurably better by liberty; but I do not believe they would be made better by liberty gained by insurrection or rebellion in the peculiar circumstances which surround them at the South. . . . Freedom, with a law and government, is an unspeakable good, but without them is a mischief. And any thing that tends to incite among men a vague insurrectionary spirit is a great and cruel wrong to them.

We must quicken all the springs of feeling in the Free States in behalf of human liberty, and create a public sentiment, based upon truths of Christian manhood. For if we act to any good purpose on the minds of the South, we must do it through a salutary and pure public sentiment in the North.

When we have corrected our own practice, and set an example of the right spirit, then we shall have a position from which to exert a beneficial public influence on the minds of Southern slaveholders. For this there must be full and free discussion. Under our institutions, public opinion is the monarch; and free speech and debate form public opinion.

If you wish to work for the enfranchisement of the African, seek to make him a better man. Teach him to be an obedient servant, and an honest, true, Christian man. These virtues are God's step-stones to liberty. . . . Truth, honor, fidelity, manhood,— these things in the slave will prepare him for freedom. It is the low animal condition of the African that enslaves him. It is moral enfranchisement that will break his bonds.

AGAINST A COMPROMISE OF PRINCIPLE.

November 29, 1860.

Crowns were once made of gold beaten out on the people's back. Now the strongest crowns are made of paper,—the paper votes of the common people.

It is always safe to be right; and our business is not so much to seek peace as to seek the causes of peace. Expedients are for an hour, but principles are for the ages.

Can any man believe that peace can come by *compromise?* It is a delusive hope. . . .

Compromises are only procrastinations of an inevitable settlement, with the added burden of accumulated interest.

OUR BLAMEWORTHINESS.

January 4, 1861.

The same thing leads to the oppression of laborers among us that leads to oppression on the plantation. The grinding of the poor, the advantages which capital takes of labor, the oppression of the farm, the oppression of the road, the oppression of the shop, the oppression of the ship, are all of the same central nature, and as guilty before God as the more systematic and overt oppressions of the plantation. It is always the old human heart that sins, North or South ; and the natures of pride and of dishonesty are universal. We have our own account to render.

I should violate my own convictions, if, in the presence of more nearly present and more exciting influences, I should neglect to mention the sins of this nation against the

Indian, who, as much as the slave, is dumb,
but who, unlike the slave, has almost
none to think of him, and to speak of his
wrongs. . . . It is a sorry commentary on a
Christian nation, and indeed upon religion
itself, that the freest and most boastfully religious people on the globe are absolutely
fatal to any weaker people that they touch.

If the Bible can be opened that all the
fiends of hell may, as in a covered passage,
walk through it to do mischief on earth, I say,
blessed be infidels!. . . . [But] wherever
the Bible has been allowed to be free, wherever it has been knocked out of the king's
hand, and out of the priest's hand, it has
carried light like the morning sun, rising over
hill and vale round and round the world ; and
will do it again!

THE BATTLE SET IN ARRAY.
April 14, 1861.

The whole lesson of the past, then, is that
safety and honor come by holding fast to
one's principles; by pressing them with

courage ; by going into darkness and defeat cheerfully for them.

Eighty years of unexampled prosperity have gone far toward making us a people that judge of moral questions by their relation to our convenience and ease. . . . And now if it please God to do that which daily we pray that he may avert,—if it please God to wrap this nation in war,—one result will follow : we shall be called to suffer for our faith. We shall be called to the heroism of doing and daring, and bearing and suffering, for the things which we believe to be vital to the salvation of this people.

On these conditions we may have peace. If we reject these conditions we are to have separation, demoralization of government, and war. . . . If you have peace, you are to stigmatize the whole history of the past ; you are to yield your religious convictions ; you are to give over the government into the hands of factious revolutionists ; you are to suppress every manly sentiment, and every sympathy for the oppressed. . . . Give me a war redder than blood and fiercer than fire, if this terrific infliction is necessary that I may maintain my faith of God in human liberty, my faith of the fathers in the instruments of liberty, my faith in this land as the appointed abode and chosen refuge of liberty for all the earth ! War is terrible, but that abyss of ignominy is yet more terrible.

THE NATIONAL FLAG. [1]

May, 1861.

A thoughtful mind, when it sees a nation's flag, sees not the flag but the nation itself. And whatever may be its symbols, its insignia, he reads chiefly in the flag the government, the principles, the truths, the history, that belong to the nation that sets it forth.

This nation has a banner, too ; and until recently wherever it streamed abroad men saw daybreak bursting on their eyes. . . . The stars upon it were to the pining nations

---

[1] Delivered to two companies of the " Brooklyn Fourteenth Volunteer Regiment," many of them members of Plymouth Church.

like the bright morning stars of God, and the
stripes upon it were beams of morning light.
As at early dawn the stars shine forth even
while it grows light, and then as the sun
advances that light breaks into banks and
streaming lines of color, the glowing red and
intense white striving together and ribbing
the horizon with bars effulgent, so, on the
American flag, stars and beams of many-
colored light shine out together. . . . It is
the banner of dawn. It means *Liberty;* and
the galley-slave, the poor oppressed conscript,
the trodden-down creature of foreign despotism, sees in the American flag that very
promise and prediction of God,—" The people
which sat in darkness saw a great light ; and
to them which sat in the region and shadow
of death light is sprung up."

How glorious, then, has been its origin !
How glorious has been its history ! How
divine is its meaning ! In all the world is
there another banner that carries such hope,
such grandeur of spirit, such soul-inspiring
truth, as our dear old American flag, made

by liberty, made for liberty, nourished in its spirit, carried in its service, and never, not once in all the earth, made to stoop to despotism! Never,—did I say? Alas! Only to that worst despotism, Southern Slavery, has it bowed! Remember, every one of you, that the slaveholders of the South, alone of all the world, have put their feet upon the American flag!

Accept it, then, in all its fullness of meaning. It is not a painted rag. It is a whole national history. It is the Constitution. It is the government. It is the free people that stand in the government on the Constitution. Forget not what it means; and for the sake of its ideas, rather than its mere emblazonry, be true to your country's flag. By your hands lift it; but let your lifting it be no holiday display. It must be advanced "*because of the truth.*"

THE CAMP, ITS DANGERS AND DUTIES.

May, 1861.

It has been the policy of this nation to discourage standing armies. It is a wise policy, and it never appeared so wise as now. Standing armies are always dangerous ; and I can hardly doubt that, had there been a hundred thousand soldiers subject to the control of the men just ejected from this government, our liberties would have been in peril. . . . The theory of our people has been, that, as the common people framed their government, administer their government, and are the sources of power and of political influence in that government, so and in like manner the common people shall be their own soldiers, and do their own fighting, when it is necessary. War will not be unnecessarily provoked when the men that provoke the war are obliged themselves to wage it.

Modes and Duties of Emancipation.
November 26, 1861.

If there be in the hand of the war-power, as John Quincy Adams thought there was, a right of emancipation, then let that be shown, and, in God's name, be employed ! But if there be given to us no right by our

Constitution to enter upon the States with a legislation subversive of their whole interior economy, not all the mischiefs of slavery, and certainly not our own impatience under its burdens and vexations, should tempt us to usurp it. This conflict must be carried on *through* our institutions, not over them. Revolution is not the remedy for rebellion. The exercise on the part of our government of unlawful powers cannot be justified, except to save the nation from absolute destruction. . . . This is not a plea against immediate emancipation ; it is but a solemn caution, lest, smarting from wrong, we seize the opportunity inconsiderately to destroy one evil by a process that shall leave us at the mercy of all others that time may bring.

THE SUCCESS OF AMERICAN DEMOCRACY.
April 13, 1862.

There are such things as American ideas, distinctive, peculiar, national. Not that they were first discovered here, or that they are entertained only here ; but because more than anywhere else they lie at the root of institutions, and are working out the laws and the policies of this people.

The root idea is this: that man is the most sacred trust of God to the world ; that his value is derived from his moral relations, from his divinity. . . . We stand in contrast with the world in holding and teaching it ; that men, having been once thoroughly educated, are to be absolutely trusted.

No pains are spared, we know, in Europe, to educate princes and nobles who are to govern. No expense is counted too great, in Europe, to prepare the governing classes for their function. America has her governing class, too ; and that governing class is the whole people. It is a slower work, because it is so much larger.

It is impossible for men who have not seen it to understand that there is no society possible that will bear such expansion and contraction, such strains and burdens, as a society made up of free educated common people, with democratic institutions.

A foreigner would think, pending a presidential election, that the end of the world had come. The people roar and dash like an ocean. "No government," he would say, " was ever strong enough to hold such wild and tumultuous enthusiasm, and zeal, and rage." True. There is not a *government* strong enough to hold them. Nothing but *self*-government will do it : that will.

Educate men to take care of themselves, individually and in masses, and then let the winds blow ; then let the storms fall ; then let excitements burn, and men will learn to move freely upon each other, as do drops of water in the ocean.

Where else was ever a government that could bear to allow entire free discussion ? We grow strong under it. Voting is the cure of evil with us. Liberty, that is dangerous abroad, is our very safety.

NATIONAL INJUSTICE AND PENALTY.
September 28, 1862.

It is important to know that the government of God over nations is conducted by an administration of natural laws. . . . It is said that natural laws are stated and immutable. That is very well for a popular expression, but it will not bear examination. For there is nothing that is less immutable than a law ; nothing that is adapted to have more elasticity ; nothing that may be more endlessly varied by the degree of intelligence that you bring to bear upon it, and the advantage which you choose to take of it. . . And the difference between civilization and barbarism is the difference between knowing how to use natural laws and not knowing how to use them.

It takes longer to make a nation accountable than an individual. But in its longer period a nation is held accountable for just exactly the same things that an individual is. For a million men have no right, because they are a million, to do what each individual one of them has no right to do, against a natural law.

The South has taken such an unfortunate

position in this war, for slavery, and she has sinned against such great light, that God is bringing down upon her condign punishment.

We, too, are suffering in the North, and in the same way that we ought to. . . . I am not making complaint against the South distinctively, but against the Nation. And by the time you have paid two thousand million dollars of taxes, and have but just begun, I think that the Lord will have got back pretty much all that the North has made out of slavery! God is a great tax-gatherer; he is out now on that errand; and he will have a prosperous time!

THE GROUND AND FORMS OF GOVERN-
MENT. November 22, 1862.

Governments are always the legitimate outworkings of the condition of those governed; and there cannot, for any prolonged period, be a government that is not, in the nature of things, adapted to those under it. . . . Governments are shadows that nations and peoples themselves cast; and they usually measure in some degree the proportions of the peoples or nations that cast them. . . . When all men are ignorant, you will have absolute monarchies ; when a part are intelligent and the rest are ignorant, you will have aristocracies ; and when the whole are intelligent, you will have democracies, or republican governments.

Republican governments cannot be had by any mere legislation. They must be the effect of compelling causes. Government is an outworking of the spirit of the people, and it holds a constant relation to their actual condition. If men are ignorant, or morally low, even under republics, they will cease to be self-governing. . . . Yet, in spite of all delays and retrocessions and plottings, unquestionably the human race is developing right on toward this final and best form of government. . . . And the tendency of the whole world at present, in every. one of its departments, is to develop the common people.

If you examine the tendency of inven- tions and mechanic arts, you shall find that,

although they work for all men, they do
not work half so much for the rich, the
strong, and the wise, as they do for the
poor, the weak, and the ignorant. . . .
There is not a truckman in New York that
does not live better than Alexander lived.
There is not a seamstress that does not have
on her table things that would have made
Queen Elizabeth stare. Take the bill of
provender, I was going to say, of Shakes-
peare's time. You might almost call it fodder,
it was so coarse, and so much like animal's
food. We should think ourselves treated
worse than the prisoners at Sing Sing, if we
had to live as the royalty did three or four
hundred years ago. They would have been
glad to live as our poor people live now, who
are clothed better than they were, who have
better houses than they had, and whose instruments of labor necessitate less drudgery
than theirs did.

And that which is true of mechanic arts is
also true of literature. If you go back to
the time of Sterne and Swift, you shall not

find, I had almost said, a single generous, humanitarian sentiment in their writings. . . . The literature of the globe to-day is humane, at least, if it is not spiritual.

More and more every year pictures are coming to be owned by persons of moderate and slender means, because they have an appetite for beauty, and must have beauty to feed it.

Once nobody could own a book unless he had a fortune. Now a man that cannot afford to own a book ought to die.

And as in respect to these elements, so in respect to learning and education. Always the rich have been able to educate their children. Not always have the poor been able to do it. But now everything is working toward the education of the common people.

Money,—will that buy you? Then stand for liberty. A slave made free will purchase a hundred dollar's worth at your factory where a slave in bondage will purchase one dollar's worth. . . . The first state of a man, like the first state of a tree, may be simplicity, and he may be, as it were, a single whip ; but as he begins to grow he will throw out branches, and these branches will throw out other branches, and those will throw out others, and he will take in more by root and leaf. Every interest that makes money and intelligence pleads for a policy of liberty.

LIBERTY UNDER LAWS.
December 28, 1862.

What, then, is Liberty,—the source or fountain of which all other liberties are but streams or defluctions ? . . . . There can be no such thing as absolute liberty,—that is, the liberty of acting according to our own wishes, without hindrance and without limitation : for man is created to act by means of certain laws. . . . As toward God, liberty means obedience to laws ; and it is only when we are disputed in the right of this obedience by men, that we begin to get an idea of liberty.

It is this obedience to law that makes such liberty safe, and gives society such benefits from it. If it was a liberty that gave a man a right to do anything that he pleased, it might be dangerous. It would then be what is in the Bible called licentiousness. But where it consists in the right of a man to follow out divine laws as they are written in him, then the more broad that liberty is, the more perfectly regulated and ordered and safe will the man's life be.

It is a serious responsibility that goes with liberty: if you have it, you must use it in the fear of God for the good of others as well as for your own good.

Speech in Manchester, England.
October 9, 1863.

Let me say one word here about the Constitution of America. It recognizes slavery as a *fact;* but it does not recognize the *doctrine* of slavery in any way whatever. It was a fact; it lay before the ship of state, as a rock lies in the channel of the ship as she goes into harbor ; and because a ship steers round a rock, does it follow that that rock is in the ship ? And because the Constitution of the United States made some circuits to steer round that great fact, does it follow that therefore slavery is recognized in the Constitution as a right or a system ?

What was it, then, when the country had advanced so far towards universal emancipation in the period of our national formation, that stopped this onward tide ? Two things, commercial and political. First, the wonderful demand for cotton throughout the world, precisely when, from the invention of the cotton gin, it became easy to turn it to service. Slaves that before had been worth from three to four hundred dollars began to be worth six hundred dollars ; that knocked away one-third of adherence to the moral law. Then they became worth seven hundred dollars,—and half the law went ; then eight or nine hundred dollars,— and there was no such thing as moral law ; then one thousand or twelve hundred dollars,—and slavery became one of the Beatitudes.

The *institutions* of America were shaped by the North ; but the *policy* of her government, for half a hundred years, by the South. . . . And now, since Britain has been snubbed by the Southerners, and threatened by the Southerners, and domineered over by the Southerners—yet now Great Britain has thrown her arms of love around the Southerners and turns from the Northerners. [*Cries of No, no!*] She don't ? I have only to say that she has been caught in very suspicious circumstances. [*Laughter and applause.*] I so speak, perhaps as much as anything else, for this very sake—to bring out from you this expression. . . . I want you to say to me, and through me to my countrymen, that those irritations against the North, and those likings for the South, that have been expressed in your papers, are not the feelings of the great mass of your nation. [*Great cheering, the audience rising.*] Those cheers already sound in my ears as the coming acclamations of friendly nations—those waving handkerchiefs are the white banners that symbolize peace for all countries. [*Cheers.*] Join with us then, Britons. [*Cheers.*] From you we learnt the doctrine of what a man was worth ; from you we learnt to detest all oppressions ; from you we learnt that it was the noblest thing a man could do *to die for a right principle.* And now, when we are set in that very course, and are giving our best blood for the most sacred principles, let the world understand that the common people of Great Britain support us.

The question was put to the South, and *with the exception of South Carolina, every State in the South gave a popular vote against secession ;* and yet, such was the jugglery of political leaders, that before a few months had passed, they had precipitated every State into secession. That never could have occurred had there been in the Southern States an educated *common people.* But the slave power cheats the poor whites of intelligence, in order to rob the poor blacks.

Against all these facts, it is attempted to make England believe that slavery has had nothing to do with this war. You might as well have attempted to persuade Noah that the clouds had nothing to do with the flood.

SPEECH IN EDINBURGH, SCOTLAND.
October 24, 1863.

If you let a steam engine, when it is full of steam, hiss at the rivets, with the scape-valve open, it cannot explode; but if the steam is shut up, and the valve closed, it will be still for a moment, and then, like thunder, it will go off! So it was in regard to this subject [Abolition of Slavery]. Those who discussed it, became convinced of its truth; but those who would not permit it to be spoken of, and shut it up, brought on explosion.

FAREWELL BREAKFAST, MANCHESTER, ENGLAND. October 24, 1863.

I do not mean merely what you mean here by the "intelligent classes." The phrase with us includes farmers, mechanics, the very bulk of our people. For it is the legitimate effect of democratic instruction, that no line can be drawn between the college-educated man at the top, and the common-school-educated man at the bottom. A thoroughly educated common people, with collegiate men to be their leaders and mouthpieces, in sympathy with them,—all moving together,— is better than any society where the bottom is ignorant, and the top is educated.

FAREWELL BREAKFAST, LIVERPOOL, ENGLAND. October 30, 1863.

It takes time for a great unorganized, and to a certain extent unvoting, public opinion, underneath institutions, to create that grand swell that lifts the whole ark up.

Great Britain is herself undergoing a process of gradual internal change. All living nations are undergoing such changes. No nation abides fixed in institutions, until it abides in death.

It is said that up to the time of the trouble of the *Trent*, England was with us, but from that time she went rapidly over the other way. That was merely the occasion, but not the cause. I understand it to have been this—that there were a great many men and classes of men in England that feared the reactionary influences of American ideas upon the internal conflicts of England herself.

There is to be a commerce yet on this globe, compared with which all we have ever had will be but as the size of the hand compared with the cloud that belts the hemisphere. There is to be a resurrection of nations ; there is to be a civilization that shall bring even that vast populous continent of Asia into new forms of life, with new demands. There is to be a time when liberty shall bless the nations of the earth and expand their minds in their own homes ; when men shall want more and shall buy more. . . . Instead, therefore, of wasting energy, peace, and manhood in miserable, petty jealousies, trans-Atlantic or cis-Atlantic, the business of England, as of America, should be to strike those key-notes of liberty, to sound those deep chords of human rights, that shall raise the nations of the earth and make them better customers be-. cause they are broader men.

I do not say that our American example will reach to the essential reconstruction of any principles in your edifice. . . . There is a latent feeling that American ideas are in natural antagonism with aristocracy. They are not. American ideas are merely these— that the end of government is the benefit of the governed. . . . And if that idea is consistent with monarchy and aristocracy, why should you fear any change ?

More than warehouses, more than ships, more than all harvests and every material form of wealth is the treasure of a nation in the *manhood of her men.* We could have afforded to have our stores of wheat burnt,—there is wheat to plant again. We could have afforded to have our farms burnt,—our farms can spring again from beneath the ashes. If we had sunk our ships,—there is timber to build new ones. Had we burnt every house,—there is stone and brick left for skill again to construct them. Perish every material element of wealth, but give me the citizen intact: give me the man that fears God and therefore loves man, and the destruction of the mere outside fabric is nothing—nothing!

How many families do I know, in which once was the voice of gladness, where now mother and father sit childless! How many heirs of wealth, how many scions of old families, well cultured, the heirs to every apparent prosperity in time to come, flung themselves into their country's cause, and died bravely fighting for it. And every such name has become a name of power, and whoever hears it hereafter shall feel a thrill in his heart,—self devotion, heroic patriotism, love of his kind, love of liberty, love of God!

HOME-RECEPTION IN BROOKLYN.
November 19, 1863.
I do not hesitate to say, what I did not say in Great Britain, that, not for any material

reason, but for a moral reason, we need her; and I say more than that, for moral reasons she needs us. For the sake of man, for the cause of God, for the hope of civilization, the two great nations of the earth, carrying a civilization which is derived from and which carries with it the common people and their uplifting in civilization—these two great Christian nations—.... let these stand together to pour out to every part of the earth the influence of Christianity, civilization, and human liberty.

FORT SUMTER FLAG-RAISING.
April 14, 1865.

Rebellion has perished. But there flies the same flag that was insulted. With starry eyes it looks all over this bay for the banner that supplanted it, and sees it not. You that then, for the day, were humbled, are here again, to triumph once and forever. In the storm of that assault this glorious ensign was often struck; but, memorable fact, not one of its *stars* was torn out, by shot or by shell. It was a prophecy!

Reverently, piously, in hopeful patriotism, we spread this banner on the sky, as of old the bow was planted on the cloud; and, with solemn fervor, beseech God to look upon it, and make it the memorial of an everlasting covenant and decree that never again on this fair land shall a deluge of blood prevail.

Rise up, then, glorious Gospel banner, and roll out these messages of God. Tell the air that not a spot now sullies thy whiteness. Thy red is not the blush of shame, but the flush of joy. Tell the dews that wash thee that thou art as pure as they. Say to the night, that thy stars lead toward the morning: and to the morning, that a brighter day arises with healing in its beams. And then, O glorious flag, bid the sun pour light on all thy folds with double brightness, whilst thou art bearing around and round the world the solemn joy—a race set free ! A nation redeemed !

A people educated and moral are competent to all the exigencies of national life.

A vote can govern better than a crown. We have proved it. A people intelligent and religious are strong in all economic elements. They are fitted for peace and competent to war. They are not easily inflamed; and when justly incensed, not easily extinguished. They are patient in adversity, endure cheerfully needful burdens, tax themselves for real wants more royally than any prince would dare to tax his people.

It is not our business to subdue nations, but to augment the powers of the common people. The vulgar ambition of mere domination, as it belongs to universal human nature, may tempt us; but it is withstood by the whole force of our principles, our habits, our precedents, and our legends.

ABRAHAM LINCOLN.

April 23, 1865.

Lincoln was a man from the common people that never forgot his kind. And now that he who might not bear the march, and the toil, and the battle with these humble citizens has been called to die by the bullet, as they were, do you not feel that there was a peculiar fitness to his nature and life that he should in death be joined with them in a final common experience to whom he had been joined in all his sympathies?

Lincoln was slain; America was meant. The man was cast down; the government was smitten at. It was the President who was killed. It was national life, breathing freedom and meaning beneficence, that was sought. . . . The blow, however, has signally failed. The cause is not stricken; it is strengthened. This nation has dissolved—but in tears only. It stands, four-square, more solid to-day than any pyramid in Egypt. This people are neither wasted, nor daunted, nor disordered. Men hate slavery and love liberty with stronger hate and love to-day than ever before. The government is not weakened, it is made stronger. How naturally and easily were the ranks closed!

Republican institutions have been vindicated in this experience as they never were before ; and the whole history of the last four years, rounded up by this cruel stroke, seems now in the providence of God to have been clothed with an illustration, with a sympathy, with an aptness, and with a significance, such as we never could have expected or imagined. God, I think, has said, by the voice of this event, to all nations of the earth, " Republican liberty, based upon true Christianity, is firm as the foundation of the globe."

CONDITIONS OF A RESTORED UNION.
October 29, 1865.

Suffrage in our community is not a privilege, or a prerogative, but a natural right. That is to say, if there is any such thing as a natural right, a man has a natural right to determine the laws that involve his life, and liberty, and property. . . . It is not giving the colored man a privilege to allow him to vote ; it is developing a long dormant natural right. He has a right to citizenship because he is a man, unless he has forfeited it by crime.

I know there are many to whom this subject is unwelcome, and who say, "It seems as though there never would be an end of this negro agitation." There are many that say, "Ever since I was born I have breakfasted, and dined, and supped upon this Negro. He is in the pulpit, in conventions, in caucuses, everywhere!" . . . . Just as quick as you are willing to trust your own American principles, just as quick as you put into practice your own American doctrine that *all men are born equal, and have inalienable rights*, he will sink out of notice as a vexation.

LETTER TO THE CLEVELAND (O.) CONVENTION. August 30, 1866.

Civilization is a growth. None can escape that forty years in the wilderness who travel from the Egypt of ignorance to the promised land of civilization. The freedmen must take their march. I have full faith in the results. If they have the stamina to

undergo the hardships which every uncivil-
ized people has undergone in its upward
progress, they will in due time take their
place among us. That place cannot be
bought, nor bequeathed, nor gained by
sleight of hand. It will come to sobriety,
virtue, industry, and frugality.

LETTER TO A PARISHIONER.
September 8, 1866.

As I look back upon my course, I see no
deviation from the straight line which I have
made, without wavering, for now thirty years
in public life, in favor of justice, liberty, and
the elevation of the poor and ignorant. . . .
Not by the luster of arms, even in a just
cause, would I seek her [the Nation's] glory,
but by a civilization that should carry its
blessings down to the lowest classes, and
nourish the very roots of society by her moral
power and purity, by her public conscience,
her political justice, and by her intelligent
homes, filling up a continent, and rearing a
virtuous and noble citizenship.

NATIONAL UNITY.
November 18, 1869.

As the Nile in its great annual rise brings down something of the soil of every formation through a thousand miles, and deposits it as slime for the sun to turn to soil and fruitfulness ; as the Mississippi with its great tributary, the Missouri, carries to the fat regions around its delta a tribute gathered from almost every point of latitude and longitude on the continent, so upon these United States, with annual deposit, come the immigrating freshets of the world. It falls upon us like mud. It shall be our richest soil. When it is aerated, and when intelligence and religion and liberty shall have penetrated it, it will be most precious.

Our institutions are the best if they are the best served ; but the poorest if poorly served. Republican institutions demand energetic and virtuous citizens.

Knowledge is that which a man knows. Intelligence is that which knows it. Knowledge bears the same relation to intelligence which invested wealth does to that spirit of enterprise which creates wealth. . . . Mere knowledge will not save men. Intelligence is a preservative force.

The problems of an old society and of a new one are not the same. Intelligence is of more value to us than high culture, though high culture may be more valuable to an old monarchy than general intelligence ; and of more value to us, by and by, than just now. It is giving eyes to the whole people to give them intelligence.

Democracy does not mean a universal level. It does not mean compulsory equality. It means equitable opportunity. . . . There is a public sentiment of the public school which is just as real, and as vital, and as despotic even, as the public sentiment of the great community ; and it is a good thing to bring down to the original starting point all the elevations and inequalities which the various forces of active life produce, and to say to all the boys, " Your feet must stand on the same level : now shoot your heads as high as you please ! "

You cannot anywhere else so ill afford to be parsimonious, and call it economy, as in the administration of your common-schools.

Secure more buildings, larger buildings, better furniture, more teachers, with ampler support (for the support of the common-school teachers, especially of women teachers, is a shame and disgrace to our civilization), with more capacity, bringing hither the noblest men and the noblest women. This is political wisdom.

Things belonging to any single State alone, and not to all the States in common, must be under the supreme disposal of that State. This simple doctrine of State Rights—not State Sovereignty—will carry good government with it through all the continent. No central government could have sympathy and wise administrative adaptation to the local peculiarities of this huge nation, couched down between two oceans, whose Southern

line never freezes, and whose Northern border never melts.

The States are so many points of vitality.
The nation, like a banyan tree, lets down a
new root where each new State is established,
and when centuries have spread this gigantic
commercial tree over a vast space, it will be
found that the branches most remote from
the center do not draw their vitality through
the long intricate passages from the parent
trunk, but each outlying growth has roots of
its own, and draws straight from the ground,
by organisms of its own, all the food it wants
without dissociating its top from the parent
branches.

PAST PERILS AND PERILS OF TO-DAY.
November 29, 1877.

The Hebrew literature is colored with intense patriotism . . . . This whole human
life on earth was to them the symbol of the
wanderings of " strangers and pilgrims " ;
and when, at length, a clear conception of
another life dawned, they called Heaven *the*

New Jerusalem. Thus the heaven and the earth, time and eternity, were dressed out in the robes of their national history.

It was a wholesome practice. It harvested every great deed and achievement of their race, and made it seed-corn for the future; it trained their children to heroism, to patriotism, to a religion which enshrined them both.

The peculiarity of our early ancestry was not that they loved liberty—everything in heaven, on earth, and in the sea does that; but they discerned the royal fact, which others had missed who threw off law to find liberty, that *by taking on law men are made free.*

Human nature is the toughest thing that man ever works on. To take four million men of an inferior race, educated in the school of slavery and, by a constitutional vote of the people, make them as if they had never been ignorant slaves, is impossible; and if men have expected it, it only shows to what overfed enthusiasm they were led.

Men *grow*; and of all growths there is nothing that grows so slowly as manhood. The reason why it grows so slowly is that there is so much of it, that it is so subtle, and that is so precious in its results—for the best things are the scarcest, and are the longest in coming to perfection.

There is a danger from suppressed repudiation. . . . And suppressed repudiation is all the more dangerous than any open and avowed repudiation. . . . Whoever tampers with established standards tampers with the very marrow and vitality of public faith.

No act of Congress can ever make one pound equal to two pounds. No act of Congress can ever make a thing inferior equal to a superior. Silver coin must be made proportionate to the value of gold, as determined in the open markets of the world. All paper currency must be convertible into gold. Any other course is to teach men to cheat by law; it is to teach honest men to cheat without knowing that they cheat; it is

to teach fraud by legislation : it is a high
crime and misdemeanor : and if men in Congress do not know it, what are they there for ?

To the Society of the Army of the Potomac. June, 1878.

Every soldier should be a citizen, every
citizen should be a soldier.   An army ought
not to be a body foreign to the community
in which it exists, but sprung from it, belonging to it, continually returning to it and pen-
etrating it with its own spirit.

Since the founding of this government, I
challenge the production of a single mischief-
making military man.   If any names are re-
called of generals who have been rash and
dangerous, in every instance they will be
found to be extemporized generals, made
out of professional politicians.   Officers and
soldiers are the very men who are above all
others friends of peace.   Caucus and Congress are bellicose ; the army it is that is a
national peace society.

This nation is indebted to the West Point Military Academy for as noble a band of graduates as the world can produce. The standard of honor is nowhere higher. Respect and reverence for law and liberty are nowhere more profound. Scrupulous fidelity to duty is nowhere more nearly a religion. . . . What university, what college, what theological seminary, can point to its two thousand graduates and say, " There has never been an instance of dishonesty in the administration of public moneys ? " The only institution in this country that can say this is that Academy.

EULOGY ON GRANT.
October 22, 1885.

First came the disbanding of the army. That was so easily done that the world has never done justice to the marvel. The soldiers of three great armies dropped their arms at the word of command, dissolved their organizations, and disappeared. To-day the mightiest force on earth ; to-morrow they were not ! As a summer storm darkens the whole heavens, shakes the ground with its thunder, empties its quiver of lightning, and is gone in an hour, as if it had never been, so was it with both armies. Neither in the South nor in the North was there a cabal of officers, nor any affray of soldiers,—for every soldier was yet more a citizen.

The tidings of Grant's death, long expected, gave a shock to the whole world. Governments, rulers, eminent statesman, and scholars from all civilized nations gave sincere tokens of sympathy. For the hour, sympathy rolled as wave over all our own land. It closed the last furrow of war, it extinguished the last prejudice, it effaced the last vestige of hatred,—and cursed be the hand that shall bring them back!

Johnston and Buckner [of the Confederates] on one side of his bier, Sherman and Sheridan [of the Federals] upon the other, he has come to his tomb a silent symbol that liberty had conquered slavery, patriotism rebellion, and peace war.

www.ingramcontent.com/pod-product-compliance
Lightning Source LLC
Chambersburg PA
CBHW030824270326
41928CB00007B/881